After the Gold Rush

Archie Satterfield

AFTER THE GOLD RUSH

J. B. Lippincott Company
Philadelphia & New York

U.S. Library of Congress Cataloging in Publication Data

Satterfield, Archie.
  After the Gold Rush.

  1. Yukon Territory—Description and travel.
2. Yukon Territory—History. 3. Satterfield,
Archie. I. Title.
F1091.S38   917.19′1′0430924   76-13642
ISBN-0-397-01142-3

Acknowledgments

The author is grateful to the following publishers, magazines and newspapers for permission to reprint previously published material in this book:

A verse from "The Spell of the Yukon" by Robert Service from *The Collected Poems of Robert Service*. Reprinted by permission of Dodd, Mead & Co., McGraw-Hill Ryerson Limited and Ernest Benn Limited.

From *Here Are the News* by Edith Josie. Copyright 1966 by Clarke, Irwin & Company Limited, and The Whitehorse Star.

Two Journals of Robert Campbell: 1808–1851 and September 1850–February 1853. Edited by John W. Todd, Jr., Seattle: The Shorey Book Store. 1958. (Uncopyrighted)

The cabin fever material is based on "Mental Health Practices in the Yukon" by A. P. Abbott and J. P. Kahoe, which appeared in the January–February 1972 issue of *Canada's Mental Health*.

This book is for two grand old men of the Yukon:

Gordon Irwin Cameron

and

Alan Innes-Taylor.

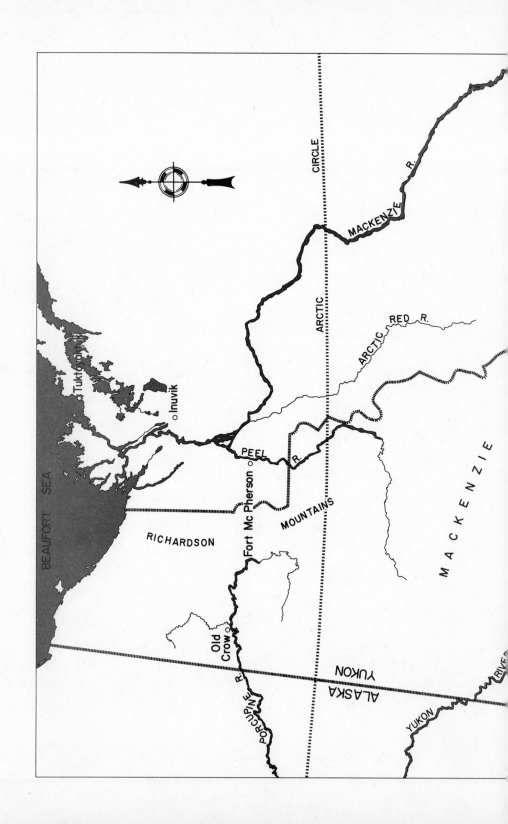

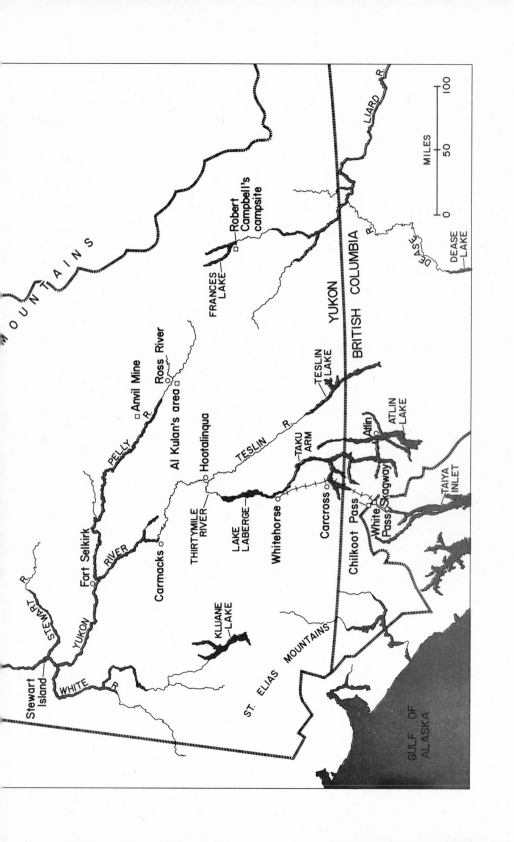

Prologue

The river had been rising steadily during the three weeks since breakup and the headwater lakes were filling with melt. Snow had left the lowlands in early May, but the ice lingered on the lakes until early June. Flowers carpeted the valley floors and new green foliage climbed hillsides up to the rockfalls beneath the granite faces of the mountains. And now we were on the swift river, drifting among rooted timber, sticks and debris swept up from the banks, silently passing trees leaning awkwardly out over the river, their roots undercut by the high water. And we watched sections of steep banks, also undercut, avalanche into the muddy, upwelling water.

During the two endless days of June we spent at Fort Selkirk, the water level dropped enough to expose the bottom of the dirt ramp that leads from the river to the high bank, and we no longer saw the trees and debris rushing past. Across from Fort Selkirk where the Pelly River silently enters the Yukon we saw a long sandbar emerge from the water like a living thing that alternately grows and disappears with the cycle of seasons.

We reloaded our boats and moved northward with the current toward Dawson City. We saw other people at the occasional highway crossing or major river intersection, but it was too early for other travelers who each year form a patchy parade during July and August. We had the river virtually to ourselves.

There was nothing unique about our journey on the Yukon, even though we liked to think so. River travel from Whitehorse to Dawson City and beyond into Alaska was no more uncommon for Yukoners than traveling across the American West on Route 66 during the first half of this century. Before the steamboats were the Indians in their moose-skin boats, canoes and rafts, then the fur traders and trappers, the prospectors and the missionaries. After the prospectors began finding gold in the tributaries, the river traffic slowly increased until the big strike of 1896 on a small stream that feeds into the Klondike River near its confluence with the Yukon.

Then the paddlewheel flotilla came, and the White Pass & Yukon Route's narrow-gauge tracks were laid over the windy Coast Range from Skagway to the downstream end of the treacherous Miles Canyon and White Horse Rapids, establishing the Yukon River as the transportation corridor from Whitehorse to the Bering Sea.

During the winter months the White Pass & Yukon Route operated a stage line that followed the river to Dawson City, and in the spring of each year for more than fifty years all travel ceased during that awkward time when the snow was gone and the ice too thin for travel. When the ice at last cleared, they launched an armada of steamboats, canoes, rowboats, skin boats and rafts called "float-me-downs" that they sold for lumber in Dawson City. Those going upstream had two choices: they either rode the steamboats that had wintered in sloughs near Dawson City, or they tracked their boats along the bank, unable to paddle against the swift current.

World War II altered the historic pattern. When the Alaska Highway was built across the bottom of the Yukon Territory in the early 1940s, spur highways soon stretched lines across the maps, heading for towns in the wilderness that few outside the Yukon had heard of and bringing others into existence. When the highway from Whitehorse to Dawson City was completed, it contained one feature that stated more bluntly than any government report could that the riverboat era was over and consigned to history. The highway engineers designed a bridge to cross the river at Carmacks too low for the high-hatted steamboats to go under. When the last steamboat on the river, the *Keno*, was taken downstream to be beached as a museum in Dawson City, the crew had to dismantle the top deck to clear the Carmacks bridge.

The highway also cleared the river of population. The woodcutters' camps strung at about 30-mile intervals had been abandoned a few years earlier when the supply of good spruce wood was depleted and the steamboats converted to oil. Now the towns disappeared too. Only a few trappers remained with the handful of privacy lovers on the 460-mile stretch between Whitehorse and Dawson City. Steamboat freight rates were so high that it was impractical to remove all household goods from cabins, unless they were moving downstream and could haul their belongings in their own boats. For years afterward river travelers could stop in cabins and find them equipped with cooking utensils and china, bedding, furniture, and such amenities as curtains over the windows and books on the shelves. But over the years the houses were gradually stripped of the furniture, and some caved in from the weight of snow. Others were weather-ravaged after windows were broken and doors left open by vandals in the wilderness.

We began, then, where most of the Yukon's history began: in the vast chain of lakes that form the headwater system in Northern British Columbia. True, there were entries from the interior of Canada by Hudson's Bay traders, and others went up the Yukon from its estuary in the Bering Sea. And during the two decades of prospecting that preceded the Klondike strike, men had wintered over at Circle City and Fortymile and Fort Reliance. But the Yukon as we know it today was settled by a south-to-north migration that began in Southern Canada and Northwestern United States, arriving by boat at Skagway, Alaska, and then over the Coast Range to Lake Bennett via the White and Chilkoot passes.

During the Klondike gold rush of 1897–98 there were several thousand—about 30,000 is the most educated guess—who survived the winter on the passes and built boats on the shores of Lake Lindeman and Lake Bennett. From there they launched more than 7,000 boats in late May 1898 and headed downstream to the Klondike.

We hiked the 32-mile Chilkoot Trail and saw the evidence of that mad winter: the abandoned townsites of Canyon City, Sheep Camp, Lindeman City; the cookstoves, boots, horseshoes and harness; the steam engine that powered an 11-mile-long aerial tramway and the tripod-shaped supports for the tramway cable; the cemeteries at Lindeman City and Bennett; the trees cut when the snow was 5 or 6 feet deep, leaving stumps nearly head-high; the tent sites dug out along the sand-bank on the shore of Lake Bennett. The more evidence we saw of the special form of madness that accompanied the gold rush, the more preposterous the whole episode became. Even in his most cynical moments, Nathanael West could not have invented a more appalling story than the Klondike. It was an event only a Dante of the North could conjure up to frighten responsible men and women into staying home in more temperate zones.

We were there in June, when the temperature ranges from 50 to 90 degrees above zero, and we slept most nights with our sleeping bags open. Those people who left so much evidence of their passing were there when the temperature dropped to 20 or 30 degrees below zero with wind that brought the chill factor down to 100 degrees below and when, in the words of one diarist, "the snow fell sideways." They suffered and died from scurvy; epidemics of spinal meningitis swept the trails. There were murders, public whippings, acts of courage and cowardice. There were avalanches that killed more than sixty stampeders in one day. And there were brilliant, warm days when the summit was packed with humanity, each person carrying load after load over the summit from Alaska into Canada, past the Mounties who lived in the blizzard-swept summit notch to collect duties and to require that each person bring 1,150 pounds of food into the country, a year's supply.

We hiked the trail, carrying no more than 40 pounds each, insulting the memory of those stampeders by having lightweight tents, comfortable hiking boots, freeze-dried food, balanced meals and the option of calling off the whole trip and flying home. We climbed over the summit in a whiteout so absolute that we felt our way over the boulders and could not see rocks bouncing down toward us when those above shouted warnings. We descended into Canada past the high sterile lakes that are free of ice less than two months a year, through the treeless alpine meadows and over perennial snowbanks, and dropped down a switchback trail into the trees again, then down another steep hill to the shore of Lake Lindeman. There we pitched horseshoes that had been left behind three quarters of a century earlier and found broken bottles, cigarette cases, belt buckles, and bones from moose, caribou, or horse steaks.

Thus we came to the river: well fed, our clothing lightweight and warm, our health in no danger of incipient scurvy. We were so far removed from the Klondike gold rush in both time and science that empathy was virtually impossible. Only geography remained the same.

Geography is the only constant in the Yukon Territory, but nearly every book written about the Yukon concerns only its history; most of those are addressed to the gold rush. Strangely, only an occasional story has appeared about the steamboat era, and little of interest has been written about other aspects of the Yukon—the Indians, the trappers, the vast wilderness: the Yukon today.

I won't presume to tell you this is a book about the entire Yukon Territory, nor is it an attempt to bring the Yukon's history up to date; that is a job for a professional historian with a research staff. But it is impossible to speak of the Yukon today without some reference to its past, and historical digressions must crop up from time to time.

In an era when Canadians are seeking a strong national identity, and when there are occasional anti-American outbursts, I cannot remember a single occasion when anyone treated me as an outsider. They accepted me, as they will anyone, on my own merits. Home addresses are of no importance in the Yukon. In return for this courtesy, I do not intend this to be a book about a foreign country. I do not understand American politics any better than I understand Canadian politics. I do not have solutions to our native problems and I cannot and will not offer solutions to those of Canada.

Rather, I am simply interested in the "nouns" of the place—the people, places and events with which I have become familiar.

Archie Satterfield

Seattle, 1976

The Headwaters

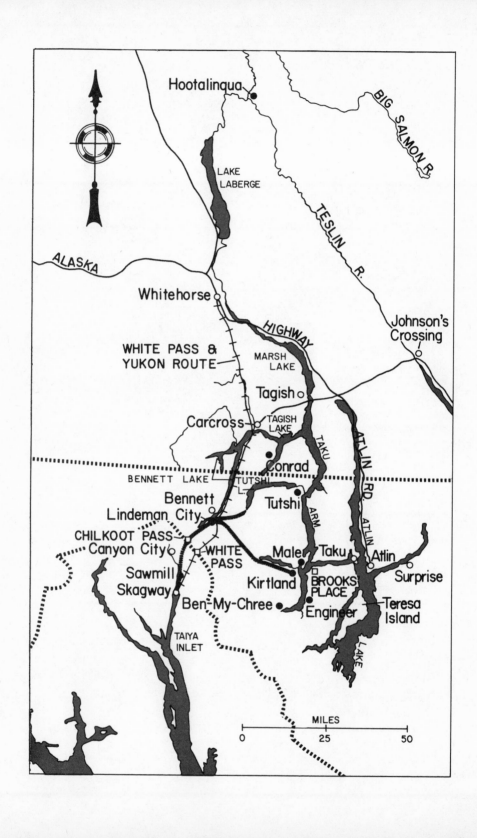

There was no wind the first morning we camped on the lakes, and when we woke a layer of fog hung suspended above the flat, dark water. We climbed the steep hill behind the tents and watched the fog slowly curl into itself—bright on the top, dark on the bottom—then shift and part as unfelt currents of air moved through it. By the time we finished breakfast most of the fog was gone and only a few strands stretched along the shores. The sun was high and hot, and the first breeze came down from the north. When we broke camp and loaded the freighter canoe a low swell was running with the steady breeze, and we ran at half-throttle to avoid taking on water. As men always have, we headed north on the lake toward the Yukon River.

The headwater lakes point northward and spill out of British Columbia across the 60th Parallel into the Yukon Territory. They are born in mountains where the meltwater trickles from snowbanks to course through alpine meadows of heather, moss and lichen and down granite rockfalls to become streams large enough to earn names, or at the broad snouts of glaciers that advance and retreat according to their own sense of time and order, birthing tan streams that too become rivers that become lakes that at last become The River.

The lakes lie beneath the mountains and glaciers that nurse them; nestled in deep valleys they have flooded beneath sheer spurs of the Coast Range. Some of the larger lakes, particularly Lake Atlin, are dotted with islands and reefs, but most are long and narrow as a fjord and devoid of visual distractions upon their surface. Glacial silt enters from the south and rapidly dissipates into the transparent moody blue that cannot be duplicated in photographs or paintings. Their beauty is so concentrated, so subtle, so subject to the climatic conditions that it is easy to become enchanted with them and consider the rest of the North mundane.

There are those who feel that way. The moving water of

the river and the frenzy of modernization that has followed the river do not appeal to them. Those who dwell on the lakeshores have learned to live at ease with the land and accept it on its own terms, while others are intent on creating an urban environment that ignores the northern latitudes and the wilderness. The lake dwellers harbor few such dreams of immortality.

The lakes are anachronisms in a time when we are concerned with vanishing wildernesses. They were used extensively by man for more than half a century, then abruptly abandoned when the steamboats were beached forever. Perhaps this makes them ineligible for wilderness as defined by purists with a misanthropic bent, but if man is considered simply another species, then those marks he has left on the shores of Lake Bennett, Lake Tagish, Lake Atlin, Grahame Inlet, Taku Arm and Marsh Lake are no more destructive than the network of game trails through the forest or the tree stumps left by beaver along unnamed feeder streams.

The lakes have a past that anyone traveling on them must inevitably accept. Their natural history stretches back to the Ice Age in speculation that is of little interest to anyone other than scholars. Instead, like an actor associated with one role or a general with one battle, most of the lakes always will be associated with the Klondike gold rush of 1897–1898 and the smaller rushes it spawned; it is virtually impossible to think of them in terms other than the part they played in that last great stampede. It is their identity. Their beauty and isolation and mute power become secondary.

While the stampeders wrote eloquently of the miseries and the heroics of the trails, they wrote almost nothing about the more spectacular beauty of the lakes. The diary entries were written almost daily during the Chilkoot and White Pass portions of the misguided migration, even though some stampeders were on the passes from September until June. Yet, when they reached the final trail camp, the entries dwindled rapidly and some made no more until they reached Dawson City ("Arrived Dawson June 23"). Perhaps the hard labor, the dangers, the masses of antlike humanity and the terrors of the trails gave them a sense of participating in history, while the journey on the lakes did not. After the last load was hauled into the last camp came the most ignoble task of all: sawing the green lumber into boards and building the boats. And the waiting. The passes were adventure, the boat-building drudgery, the waiting excruciation.

The North sometimes stimulates heroic efforts, and occasionally the mania for historical authenticity strikes otherwise reasonable men and women who become obsessed with duplicating some event from history. One such man, a rather solitary individual who had convinced himself he was born in the wrong century (many such people find their way to the Yukon), spent one long, hard summer as a total stampeder intent upon reliving the Klondike experience. He dressed in the Klondike manner, with coarse woolen clothing and high laced rubber boots, and he carried a blanket roll but no modern pack-frame or freeze-dried and dehydrated food. He traveled alone, packing nearly 1,000 pounds of food and tools over Chilkoot in relays to the shore of Lake Lindeman, which connects with Lake Bennett by a boulder-strewn stream. He became ill and holed up beside the trail in his damp bedroll until the fever passed. He felled the tough lodgepole pine, snaked them to the lake, split the scrawny trees into rough boards and built himself a blunt-ended scow about 12 feet long and 4 or 5 feet wide. He stepped a crude mast, sewed a square sail of canvas and wrestled the unwieldy vessel into the lake. He ran the rapids to Lake Bennett, then sailed and rowed down Bennett, Tagish and Marsh, and drifted down the river to Lake Laberge, where the rowing and sailing continued for another 30 miles until he was at last free of the lakes. He arrived in Dawson City just before freeze-up that fall, beached the scow, and quietly went away. Someone in Dawson City moved the scow to a vacant lot several blocks from the river and left it as another monument to the folly (or determination, depending on one's point of view) so common in the Yukon.

Yukoners tend to accept such actions without derogatory comment, whether they understand them or not. There is an old code of ethics which states that Above Sixty one must not steal or kill and to hell with all other laws. This simplicity of social order—which may have been only a wish anyway—has yielded to the inevitable bureaucracy that follows the frontier as surely as schools and churches, but enough of the old tolerance for idiosyncrasies remains to permit people to become temporary relics from another time.

While the stampeders considered the lakes an inconvenience, a barrier to be crossed, their very size demands one's attention. Lake Atlin is the largest natural lake in British Columbia and is more than 60 miles long. Taku Arm is nearly as long but much narrower; Bennett is 26 miles long, Marsh and Tagish about the same. Windy Arm, an accurately named spur off Tagish Lake, is the smallest at some 12 miles, but its narrow, walled configuration has given it a reputation of being the roughest of the group due to the winds that fall off the mountains and are compressed into the narrow corridor, creating waves 6 feet high or more.

Of the group, Lake Bennett has been used the most. Its maidenhead was taken a century ago by the lure of instant wealth along the Yukon River. But like some women upon whom men regularly force their attentions, Lake Bennett has held up well and its dramatic beauty is intact. Several thousand people have traveled its length, steamboats once paddled up and down it while the White Pass & Yukon Route tracks were being laid between it and Whitehorse, and more recently by those retracing the route from tidewater at Skagway, Alaska, to the Klondike area at Dawson City.

On the lake one must accept the wind that blows through much of the day and night, alternately pouring off the Coast Range and blowing off into the north, or being sucked back over the mountains toward the Gulf of Alaska's storm system, an inhaling and exhaling with almost the predictability of a living thing. It is at its best early in the morning before the trains and the wind arrive and again in the evening after they are gone. Then you can look downlake to the north and see the granite mountains with steep walls and rounded, barren tops repeating themselves in absolutely flat water the color of an Irish girl's eyes. During the absolutely still periods between the winds, the silence is so complete that the sudden feeling of isolation makes one seek out sound again, and one catches oneself becoming boisterous or moving closer to the stream

22

that connects Bennett and Lindeman for the reassurance of sound.

About midway down the lake, where the 60th Parallel crosses, the western shore opens up to show West Arm running directly back to the foot of the main Coast Range with the glacier-clad mountains standing silent and forbidding. An otherwise beautiful day on the lake receives a sobering note by the appearance of the range standing aloof and unyielding as an eagle above the blues and greens. It is a reminder, of which there are many in the Yukon, that summer is transitory, that this is essentially a land of winter.

Dominating the Bennett area is the shell of a log church with a steeple on the crest of a low but steep hill that looks north down the lake. Every day since the turn of the century the White Pass & Yukon Route trains have disgorged passengers and crews for lunch at the dining room on the southern end of the lake. Even though it is still Canada—British Columbia to be exact—the American and Canadian crews exchange places on the trains here. When they have time, passengers hike up the hill to look inside the church and read the almost obliterated sign beside the front door that says it was a Presbyterian Church begun in 1899, then abandoned. Apparently during the railroad construction a minister appeared on the scene and verbally flailed his flock into building the log church, complete with intricate designs of native timber, branches, and twigs. Then, when the shell was completed, the congregation departed and the minister was left alone on the hill as the steamboats made their last runs and the innkeepers, café owners and dentists boarded the train and followed the tracks north.

Just below the church, with an equally commanding view of the lake, is a cluster of buildings ranging in size from three or four of standard outhouse design, but without the attending odor, to a large cabin built of rough-sawn lumber rather than the usual logs. On its side is a professionally painted sign that identifies it as TRAPPER DAN'S. For one summer it was occupied by two young men who halfheartedly tried to convince people there actually was a man named Trapper Dan who roamed the subarctic bush throughout the year and came there to roost each winter. One of the occupants wore a bushy beard and glasses over solemn eyes, the other wore neat town clothes and no beard. They sold, or rather tried to sell, candy bars, gum, "glacier-cooled pop," battered railroad spikes painted gold with LAKE BENNETT, B.C., printed on them, postcards with hand-drawn northern scenes, film, cigarettes, and a few old bottles dug out of the refuse heap nearby.

They introduced themselves as Henry Wilkins (bearded) and Russ Devine (nonbearded), the former from England, the latter from Eastern Canada—and both possessed by that pleasant, nonfatal malady known as northern mañana. Neither was given to sudden acts or motions, and when they did move it was with the utmost economy. Both were anxious to receive mail from the noon train, yet when it came they waited more than an hour before strolling down the hill to the railroad buildings to retrieve it. There is always time in the perpetual light where tomorrow is only an extension of today and yesterday.

They lived in Carcross, at the northern end of the lake, but were trying to avoid going back to mining and other hard-labor jobs by becoming a tourist attraction at Bennett. They weren't doing well because the railroad didn't give passengers enough time for a meal and a long stroll, and their plan of selling souvenirs and munchables was not materializing.

Henry was quietly persistent, though, and he painted a few signs by hand when he wasn't busy painting spikes and postcards. When the trains were due, he loaded the signs in his canoe and paddled out near the railroad, where he held up the signs, one by one, that proclaimed CANDY, POP, CIGARETTES and other temptations. His sign flashing was frequently interrupted by the unstable canoe, treating passengers to the sight of a serious Henry, with a Buster Keaton solemnity, rocking wildly back and forth or paddling frantically when the wind pushed him too close to the rocky shore and old piling stubs left from the steamboat docks. He almost swamped several times, and elderly women on the train would hold their hands over their mouth in fear for him.

Trapper Dan's lasted only one summer. Russ went to work as a house painter and Henry for the company that runs a fuel oil pipeline from Skagway to Whitehorse. Henry also became the Carcross correspondent for the *Whitehorse Star* and began writing an adventure novel. The sign remains on the cabin at Bennett, beckoning tourists to an establishment that no longer exists. If the sign survives vandals and wood gatherers over the years, perhaps a mythology will grow from it and historians will ponder it as they do the Klondikers' debris—now called artifacts—left behind on Chilkoot.

The narrow-gauge tracks run the entire length of the eastern shore, snaking alternately along the narrow bank beneath the mountains and through gaps blasted from the stubborn granite, then leave the lakes behind at Carcross. Before the gold rush Carcross was a small off-again-on-again Tagish Indian village, the site selected because the fishing was good in the shallow, sluggish stream that empties Lake Bennett into Tagish Lake. Here the woodland caribou used the stream as a crossing—hence the present name, a contraction of Caribou Crossing. It is here, too, that the White Pass & Yukon Route tracks cross, giving a permanence to the village beyond its wild food value.

Carcross looks as though a Hollywood crew moved in to make a film—a northern *Bad Day at Black Rock* or perhaps a *Shane*—and left day before yesterday. It is dominated by two brightly painted buildings, Matthew Watson's two-toned brown general store and the black-and-white Caribou Hotel on the west side of the tracks. On the opposite side is the utilitarian and well-used railroad station, the paddlewheeler *Tutshi*, the tiny steam engine named *Little Duchess*, and a restored wagon used by the railroad during the steamboat era. These buildings and museum pieces stand out sharply against the sheer mountains behind Carcross and look at once incongruous and esthetically pleasing. One suspects they were placed for the sake of convenience rather than overall appearance, but it is doubtful that a professional designer could have arranged them more attractively.

For a number of years Carcross was a major intersection for transportation and tourism. The railroad operated a gracious, efficient tour system that brought several thousand clients north every summer. They came by cruise ship up the Inside Passage to Skagway, where they stayed at least one night in the rambling Pullen House, operated by a widow who arrived in Skagway at the height of the gold rush and stayed on to become one of Alaska's most famous and respected hostesses. Then the tourists rode the train over White Pass to Bennett for the inevitable roast beef lunch that has been served family style for decades, then on to Carcross.

They left the train at Carcross and boarded the *Tutshi*, one of the smaller paddlewheelers built especially for the headwater lakes, and began a leisurely cruise down the interconnecting lakes through what is without question some of the most beautiful scenery in North America. A typical trip included a stop at the mining town of Conrad on Windy Arm, back up the lake, and then down the narrow Taku Arm to its very tip beneath the Juneau Icecap. There they walked a long pier built over the muddy glacial silt to Ben-My-Chree, a horticulturalist's dream in a very unlikely place. Ben-My-Chree began as a mine up in the mountains near the glaciers, but when it caved in, the owners never reopened it. Instead, a couple from the Isle of Man named Partridge established themselves on the rich soil and began growing vegetables and flowers. They imported evergreen trees and shrubs from various parts of the world, and soon made the place a high point of steamboat trips. Some stayed overnight while the boats went to Taku and back. They served tea, crumpets and rhubarb wine, and guests were free to roam the landscaped hills and bottomlands. The Partridges never tired of explaining to guests that Ben-My-Chree meant "girl of my heart" in their native language of Manx. After the Partridges died—within six months of each other—the railroad took over and maintained the place for tourists until the steamboat era ended.

From Ben-My-Chree, the *Tutshi* steamed majestically up Taku Arm to the Engineer Gold Mine, which was always an almost-but-never-quite successful operation, then into Grahame Inlet, which runs due east from Taku Arm. At the end of the narrow inlet, the *Tutshi* was unloaded at the Taku railroad station, where the *Little Duchess* ran on a narrow-gauge track 2 miles up the Atlin River to Scotia Bay on Lake Atlin. It was the shortest railroad in North America at the time, and so elemental that it ran forward one way, reverse the other, and passengers and freight were mixed almost at random on the small open cars. At Scotia Bay another steamship picked up the passengers and freight for a run across to the tiny picture postcard town of Atlin. After a stay in a hotel there, the tourists retraced the route back to Carcross, caught the train to Whitehorse to board the riverboats for the trip downriver to Dawson City, returned the same way to Whitehorse, took the train back to Skagway to catch a ship back home. While tourism is still the mainstay of the Yukon, second only to mining, no more leisurely and varied tour packages have been organized since the steamboats stopped.

Today, Carcross has an air of patient waiting to it, and even when cars are seen on its street that dead-ends at the lake, there is that air of subdued expectancy, much like remnants of the cargo culture in the South Pacific, still waiting for the ship to come in. Unfortunately, Carcross's ship came in, and stayed. The *Tutshi* stands high and dry for the swallows to nest in and for the federal government to restore and paint as a tourist attraction again. As with many towns in the Yukon, Carcross has a subdued melancholy to its atmosphere, and when hilarity bubbles up from the silence of its outpost setting, it has the characteristics of diversion. Afterward the town settles back to its timeless, patient waiting.

Its most famous citizens lie buried in the cemetery across the stream from town where most of the Indians live. Although it is nearly six hundred miles from the Klondike, occupants of three graves figured prominently in the gold rush: Skookum Jim and his sister Kate and their cousin Tagish Charley. Skookum Jim, Tagish Charley, and Kate's husband, a white man named George Washington Carmack, made the great discovery on August 16, 1896, while on a fish-netting expedition in the Klondike River. After they became wealthy, Carmack took his wife Outside to Seattle, where she became famous for throwing wads of cash from her hotel window to watch the scrambling below. And when she first checked into a hotel, she blazed a trail from the lobby to her room with an ax. Eventually Carmack abandoned her for a white woman, and Kate returned to

Carcross to live out the rest of her life, bitter with her dreams of what could have been.

Skookum Jim continued prospecting even though he was wealthy, eventually wearing himself out in search of the mother lode. Tagish Charley, because of his wealth, came to be treated as if he were white. He owned the Caribou Hotel in Carcross and was one of the few Indians permitted to drink like a white man. He gave big dances in his home across the stream from town and spent much of his time at the bar in his hotel. One afternoon while walking home across the railroad bridge, he toppled off into the cold water and drowned.

Today the hotel is owned by an unflappable, pleasant woman named Dorothy Hopcott. She does not pretend the Caribou is anything other than what it is: an aging hotel built for comfort. Like all buildings in the Yukon, it has double doors in the entry to create a dead-air space for insulation in all seasons. On the left side of the well-worn entryway, opposite the dark bar, is the café, with a few unsteady tables, some cluttered with newspapers and magazines, and about six stools at the counter. Like the entryway, the café is well used but comfortable, and the bright summer sun filters through double panes of glass onto an assortment of potted plants. The overall effect is reminiscent of old cafés in the American desert which double as living rooms for the owners.

For several decades a tall, roomy bird cage stood near the front window inside of which lived a scruffy, colorful parrot who seemed to divide its time between glaring at diners and burying its head beneath a wing, only to pull it out again and mutter like an absentminded, lonely old man speaking of things only he remembered. Had the parrot lived in a more heavily populated area, its existence and death would have gone unnoticed; but, because it was a tropical bird—a very old one—living in the subarctic, it was something of a celebrity to writers wandering through the Yukon. So its death in 1972 became a national event.

It was simple for Mrs. Hopcott: the bird had died and she would bury it and that would be that. But, earlier, a writer for the Canadian Press wire service named Dennis Bell had written a humorous story about the parrot that appeared in newspapers across North America, and Bell now saw an opportunity to create more interest in the incongruous bird.

He wrote that "the world famous Carcross parrot, reputedly the oldest, meanest, dirtiest bird north of the 60th Parallel, has chomped his last cracker," and that the bird was found deceased, drumsticks up, after having survived the ferocious northern blizzards, fire, and the dregs of the Klondike gold rush.

The parrot—predictably known as Polly, although its gender apparently was never established for certain—arrived in Carcross sometime after the gold rush. Its first recorded owner was a Captain Alexander who operated a mine near Carcross. Alexander and his wife left Polly at the Caribou Hotel in 1918 to take a trip Outside aboard the Canadian Pacific's steamer *Princess Sophia*, and they perished when the ship foundered between Skagway and Juneau. Polly stayed on at the hotel, one of the fixtures that remained with the hotel whenever it changed ownership.

For years Polly was known as a hard drinker, and it delighted patrons of the hotel bar to feed the bird liquor until it got so drunk it would fall off its perch and lie on the bottom of the cage with its feet up in the air—another victim of alcohol, the North's major social problem.

Mrs. Hopcott said that several years ago—and she isn't sure why—Polly quit drinking liquor. One of its owners also taught it several verses of "Onward, Christian Soldiers" and eliminated much of its racy vocabulary and salacious sea chanties. The cantankerous old bird stopped talking to adults, except when asked if it wanted a cracker: its answer invariably was "Go to hell." Polly seemed to appreciate children, however, and sometimes would hold long conversations with toddlers, which consisted mainly of incomprehensible mutterings the children seemed to understand.

When Polly died, a local chiropractor declared it the victim of a heart attack. Mrs. Hopcott put its remains in a tiny cardboard coffin lined with red velvet, placed the coffin in a deep freeze until spring when the ground thawed sufficiently for a proper burial and assumed the matter was closed.

It probably would have been had Polly died in the summer. But during the long winter there is little for Yukoners to do for recreation other than have house parties, watch television and drink. When the news of Polly's death reached Whitehorse, there was an immediate demand for a proper funeral, although the ground was frozen granite-hard. Matters were taken out of Mrs. Hopcott's hands, and the funeral became a territorywide function. The citizens decided Polly rated a state funeral, and Commissioner James Smith granted special permission to bury the bird just inside the gate of the hallowed ground of the Carcross cemetery.

A special car for mourners was placed on the southbound train from Whitehorse, and services were held up at least an hour because some governmental dignitaries were late in arriving by car.

Standing in the below-freezing air of noon, the large gathering assembled around the tiny coffin. Rather than a minister—nobody seemed certain a minister would officiate, and they didn't really want one anyway—an elderly Indian named Johnny Johns performed the eulogy. He sang several choruses of "I Love You Truly," accompanying himself on a skin drum, while his wife stage-whispered the words when he forgot them or interrupted when he got them wrong. The musical portion of the ceremony complete, Johnny doffed a hundred-year-old tribal ceremonial hat made of swan feathers in a special tribute.

When the funeral ended and Polly was placed beneath the frigid ground, the entire population of Carcross, part of Whitehorse, and other communities bellied up to the bar in the Caribou Hotel and held a long, loud wake.

Again Mrs. Hopcott thought the matter was closed—and again she was wrong. Replacements, none solicited, soon arrived from donors. The first was described as a cross between a turkey vulture and a bird of paradise. Named Scarlet O'Hara, this parrot was given by an elderly woman who said Scarlet had belonged to the captain of the H.M.S. *Hood*, the big British battlewagon that was sunk while Scarlet was on shore leave.

The second, a younger bird, arrived and was named Polly II. It had the disquieting habit of hanging upside down from the perch, then dropping like a stone to land on its head, which led Mrs. Hopcott to wonder if someone might have given her a defective bird.

The Canadian Press story had been picked up by newspapers all over the continent and appeared in other papers throughout the British Commonwealth. A disk jockey from New Orleans interviewed Mrs. Hopcott several times by telephone, then sent her an unasked-for autographed photo of himself, which puzzled her: "Why would I want that?" she asked.

A parrot fancier from British Columbia explained the best method of housebreaking new birds: "They must be locked in with affection. Take him up only when he rootsie-toots. When it is time for him to do droppings, put him on his perch and say 'Rootsie-toots, Polly.' The moment he does it, pick him up and pet him to display your pleasure. You will be surprised how quickly he learns."

Mrs. Hopcott stuck with the tried-and-true newspaper at the bottom of the cage, in part because it was simpler—and, one suspects, in part because she did not care to stand near customers singsonging "Rootsie-toots, Polly," and then explaining to diners what she was attempting to do. But the expression found its way into the Yukoners' vocabulary and one can occasionally hear someone in Whitehorse excusing themselves from a bar with those words.

While Carcross dozes through the lopsided seasons with an occasional event to stimulate winter conversation, Atlin, at the opposite end of the old lake steamboat route, appears to be slowly awakening. It, too, is served by a spur off the Alaska Highway that dead-ends just beyond town, making Atlin a destination rather than a way station while enroute elsewhere. If Carcross has the appearance of just happening into existence, a fluke of geography, Atlin looks more intentional. It is as though its founder paddled the length of the lake and decided on the townsite for no more practical reason than it was the most beautiful he could find.

Of course wilderness towns have never been established for esthetic reasons. Atlin appeared because it was close to the creeks where gold was found and where the future inland ghost town of Surprise was built. Atlin grew because it was on a cove of the lake with deep water and protection from the weather, and only after the gold mining petered out did its beauty become a factor in its survival. The beauty today is heightened by the 60-mile drive down the narrow, twisting dirt road that gives no suggestion of beauty until the last hill is descended and the cluster of false-front buildings can be seen below and Atlin Mountain rises up on the far shore with a series of stepping-stone islands leading toward it across the broad, brooding lake.

Atlin leaves the impression of being unpretentious and at ease with itself. Its low-profile buildings are spread casually across a low hill that gives most houses a view of the lake and mountains. Some blocks are composed of tiny cabins clustered tightly together, as if for reassurance, while other blocks have only one or two buildings, or none.

The pace is quiet and slow, something like a town in the American South or in the tropics. People do not hurry anywhere; they stroll or amble in observance of the northern mañana ethic.

Although there are always other people around, one can feel overwhelmed by the scenery in Atlin; there is a more pronounced sense of standing at the edge of an endless wilderness than in the other towns without such a spectacular view of the surroundings. The lake's western shore is defined by a mountain range, but the eastern shore undulates off into the infinity of Canada's interior where maps are devoid of all but a maze of lakes and rivers across the entire continent.

The turn-of-the-century stores and public buildings, the steamboat *Tarahane* on a cradle at the lake's edge and a tall clock outside the post office stopped at 11:25 give Atlin the hush of a museum, as though history itself stopped with the clock. Even the occasional sound of a motorboat or float plane does not fill the curious void that space and timelessness create. On the contrary, a few familiar sounds tend to heighten the isolation. We become accustomed to living our lives within boundaries more rigid than we realize. The freedom of space without obvious limits gives us the vulnerability of a man released from prison. Geography subjugates human activity and it becomes easier to understand why man, apparently the only creature with ambitions toward immortality, often feels compelled in such surroundings to erect monuments to himself—pyramids in the jungles and deserts, public buildings, highways and dams in the Arctic. It is also easier to understand why we speak in terms of conquering the wilderness. We appear determined to make nature take us seriously, to extract a tithe from the land and to leave our graffiti forever drawn on the landscape.

The Atlin area is not conducive to inflated egos. The wilderness around it does not seem to need us to oversee its welfare, and our absence would not leave a vacuum. Nothing, one suspects, would change should we become extinct.

We spent four days on the inland sea in a freighter canoe and saw neither man nor building. We crossed the lake from Atlin and entered the long, narrow Torres Channel between the western shore and Teresa Island with mountains towering on both sides. Broad sandy beaches stretched back to the timber and pure streams emptied into the lake. At the southern end of Teresa Island a maze of smaller islands began, with many tiny bays and coves to confuse us as we sought the passage back to the open lake. The water was flat and we regretted having to use a motor, and when we at last chose a campsite on a gravel beach, the silence was so intense that two of the children said they could hear only the ringing in their ears.

We saw only an occasional cow moose living on the islands with its calves until fall, and no spoor of boaters—beer bottles, cigarette filters, plastic bags, film wrappers or even dead campfires. It turned cool after dinner and the sun hit only the tops of mountains. We built a large bonfire and sat silently before it, our lives suddenly so basic that we knew nothing of importance worth uttering.

The next day we continued south on the lake to the very end where a high-walled neck of water called Llewellyn Inlet leads back to a trail head. A narrow beach beneath low-growing spruce gave protection from the wind that had come up and was sending 3- and 4-foot waves crashing against the sheer walls of the inlet. We found a plaque with a blue background and white lettering that identified it as the Stewart James Trail that leads back to Llewellyn Glacier. The reverse side of the plaque identified it as an oil-company sign recycled into a memorial for the man who once led visitors over the trail, some as famous as the late Eddie Cantor.

We followed the rough trail through wind-contorted spruce and low brush over a steep ridge that opens up to a broad, flat plain about a half mile wide between two low glacier-scarred mountains where the ice once flowed. It since has receded far back toward the summit of the Coast Range to leave the gravel-strewn moraine flat as an airfield with a tan river winding leisurely toward the lake. At the west end of the plain was the broad, dirty snout of the beached glacier, its life slowly draining away.

If the silence and space of the wilderness can make one uneasy, contemplating the amoral power of glaciers can be terrifying. Scientists are issuing more frequent warnings that not only is another ice age almost a certainty; it can arrive with a suddenness measurable in generations rather than centuries. As one stands beneath the snout of a glacier and remembers that Whitehorse once was under ice more than a mile thick, and that in other parts of the North mastodons were found perfectly preserved in the ice, the ego becomes bruised. Concepts of land ownership and the territorial imperative seem futile.

The glaciers, the wilderness, the climate and the lakes all command total respect. Although one constantly hears the old-timers uttering the old chestnuts that "to survive you must live with the land," or that "you accept the land on its own terms," they have not acquired the rust of a cliché. The mirrored surface of the lakes can change rapidly into deep, uneven swells with vicious cross-chops that create freak waves and "holes" to swamp boats. The water temperature hovers only a few degrees above freezing and, combined with the wind that ricochets the chill factor up and down at all seasons, it makes swimming long distances to shore unlikely. The weather itself is incredibly unstable beneath the icecap. Regional forecasts can never take into account the sudden showers, the strong winds or even those rare, absolutely still days created by the meeting of the dry inland weather and the damp storm system from the Gulf of Alaska a few miles over the mountains.

We returned to Atlin for motor repairs and to hire a guide to run the 2-mile-long but treacherous Atlin River. We stayed in a cabin owned by Tom Kirkwood, who came to Atlin nearly thirty years earlier with a butcher named James Smith. Kirkwood bought the weekly newspaper and Smith worked in a butcher shop, married a local girl and moved to Whitehorse to manage a grocery store. A few years later he was appointed Commissioner of the Yukon. Kirkwood seems pleased for Smith's success, but certainly not envious. He is not anxious to see Atlin become a major tourist destination and actually discourages group rates for his cluster of cozy log cabins on the lake shore.

Atlin is still far enough off the normal tourist routes to retain its isolation. It had a brief, intense gold rush in 1898–1899 that was overshadowed by the Klondike rush. The Atlin stampede failed to attract the colorful personalities and chroniclers who made Dawson City rather eccentric, and its gold on creeks east of the lake failed to create much interest outside the North.

A few stampeders followed the all-water route from Bennett and Carcross, but most followed the White Pass Trail to the summit, then swung east on the Fan Tail Trail down a stream to Fan Tail Lake, and along its outlet to the major lake system. Small, hopeful towns were built where the trail ended on Taku Arm, but their lives were unmercifully short.

So was the rush. The professionals soon arrived with dredges and blank checks and deed forms to buy the mining claims. Atlin began a slow population drain until it bottomed out at about 150, mostly middle-aged couples and elderly bachelors, and the population stayed at that level until the early 1970s. Its mining era was relatively staid among the gold rush towns. Except for a few incidents over claims, which were common everywhere, Atlin was very orderly. It had an operatic society that performed Gilbert and Sullivan, and ice boating was a popular winter activity. Like most frontier towns, it was built of wood that soon became tinder-dry in the semiarid climate. Most of its buildings were burned in one fire or another and a collection was taken to buy a fire engine, on which runners were installed so it could navigate the streets during the winter. Atlin had virtually no transportation or communication after the lakes froze and the steamboats were docked for the winter. Trips were made to other towns occasionally by dog team and a winter stage service, powered by horses or dogs, ran on a sometime basis. Carcross was its exit to the Outside, and still is to a large extent for those who travel by boat to catch the train to Whitehorse or Skagway. During the late 1930s a floatplane service was established by a nonchalant, resourceful pilot named Frank Barr. He flew a Fairchild Pilgrim for several years, barely earning enough to buy gasoline and food. After the spur from the Alaska Highway was built, Atlin's population began a slow upward climb, and the median age a slow descent with the arrival of couples with children. Because the area is so beautiful, even residents of other towns speak of Atlin with both respect and envy, and there is something of a protective attitude toward it.

If Atlin looks idyllic to the casual visitor—as most small, isolated towns in a beautiful setting do—Joe and Carol Florence say it really is. They are an energetic couple with two lively small boys who have not lost their awe of the wilderness they can see from their home on the lake. They say they discovered Atlin because Carol had a headache while they were driving up the Alaska Highway. They went down to Atlin for an aspirin and were looking for a place to buy before they left town. They returned to their home in Twin Falls, Idaho, sold everything, moved to Atlin and started a boat service. Joe had learned something about operating boats on whitewater in Hells Canyon; he spent the first summer roaring around Lake Atlin and up and down Atlin River, and later he went into business hauling passengers and delivering packages for the sprinkling of people who live on the lake system during the summer.

Joe runs a trapline on a snowmobile, pulling a sled behind with a float attached to a long line so he can find everything should he drop through the ice. He doesn't say how he would get out of the lake himself: one problem at a time.

As with all who love the North, Joe and Carol look forward to the winters. The frantic pace of summer with the mosquitoes and other penalties of warm weather disappear and life takes on a more leisurely, subdued pace. Those who accept the severe seasons are usually those who do not live in the larger towns and whose work is more closely related to their natural environment. The Florences can sit in their high-ceilinged living room with the fireplace crackling behind them and watch wolves play on the frozen lake. Sometimes they see a moose stroll across their yard and through town; and they say the snow and ice seem to hold the light and it is seldom completely dark even on moonless winter nights.

Not everyone feels so at ease with their surroundings. It is often more difficult for those in an urban environment to accept the long, cold winter nights, and it is usually these who attempt to live as though they were in more temperate zones. The long nights of winter and long days of summer constitute an inconvenience. Children resist going to bed in broad daylight and become restless when they are confined to the house during extremely cold weather. Since most homes are by necessity small to conserve heating costs, winter can lead to short tempers among people who cannot learn to accept the conditions of such extreme latitudes.

It is called cabin fever in the North and the "housewife syndrome" in Canada's prairie provinces. It is a joke to all except those who have fallen victim to it; many in northern and western Canada have. Yet many old-timers have never experienced it and say they do not believe in it—that, if it does exist, the only cure is to keep occupied. Little research has been done on the subject, perhaps because the old-timers' antidote is the only known cure. But it does exist and is considered a major problem by social workers and psychiatrists assigned to the North. Today most victims are women—housewives—but in the past, when men lived alone in the tiny cabins on mining claims or near game trails, they often shared their lonely lives with a partner. If the partnership survived the first winter, it was generally assumed it could continue almost indefinitely.

There are stories, some comic and some tragic, about those who did not survive a winter. Some men stopped speaking to each other in November but remained in the tiny cabin together until breakup in June, which leads one to wonder if the term breakup might not originally have applied to partnerships as well as the clearing of lake and river ice. Some silent partnerships resulted in carefully defined territories, and the men drew lines, both real and imaginary, down the center of the cabin from the door to the opposite wall, through the single stove. Neither man crossed the line. Sometimes these divisions occurred when one man had an irritating habit, such as whistling through his teeth or humming or talking too much or not enough. When spring breakup came, they would split the gear and part in silence. Sometimes the men went to extremes in the gear division and sawed boats in half rather than permit the other to own it. They even split sacks of flour in half, ruining all of it rather than dividing sacks evenly. There was an occasional murder, but surprisingly few. A recent case occurred near Pelly Crossing when two men from a northern state moved into a cabin for the winter as a lark. They happily cleaned up the cabin and area around it and built themselves a small brewery for something to occupy themselves as well as provide refreshment. After winter came they found themselves drinking the beer faster than they could brew it, so they took turns driving the few miles to the roadhouse at Pelly Crossing to visit and bring back several cases of professionally brewed beer.

Tempers soon began flaring and silence set in. One set up a wall tent away from the cabin and moved in, and all conversation ended. However, they kept brewing what beer they could and took turns making the trip to Pelly Crossing. The partnership ended long before winter did. One quietly packed up, drove to the highway—and kept going. Several days later, when it was obvious he was completely alone, the other walked to a nearby house, caught a ride to Whitehorse, and left the Yukon, too.

Most men alone do not seem to suffer ill effects from solitude, and return to town each spring no more odd than when they left the previous fall. Old-timers are careful to point out that these men are alone but not lonely. They are occupied the entire winter and they are alone by choice. There aren't many such men who winter over in the bush alone today, but for several decades it was an ordinary way of life. For half a century the river was lined with woodcutters in their camps and telegraph operators from Ashcroft, B.C., all the way to Dawson City, nearly always men alone going about their chores of providing wood for the steamboats and keeping the telegraph lines repaired and sending messages.

The woodcutters were strung along the river at roughly 30-mile intervals, and their job was to keep on hand at least enough wood for a season, sticks 4 feet long, dried and cured one year before use. White Pass & Yukon Route supplied them with tools and a horse to snake fallen trees out of the forest. All year long they kept busy chopping down trees, trimming off the branches, then hitching the horse to them and dragging them into camp. They sawed them into the 4-foot lengths, split the wood, and piled it near the bank. They kept up to two hundred cords of wood stacked at a time, and when the timber was depleted in one area, White Pass moved them to another.

Many of these men led lives nearly as difficult and monastic as a Trappist. Some almost never went to town, and most never returned to their homes for a visit. A few would make two or three trips a year to visit a prostitute—one was addicted to black prostitutes and when the last one in Dawson City died, he had to go all the way back to Skagway—but they apparently were the exception. Some had extensive libraries and continually surprised the rare visitor with their grasp of world events: their views were not cluttered with the daily news; rather, they received so little news that a broader perspective on events was easier. When visitors did come, the woodcutters were pleased to see them, but usually one night of talk was enough and they were equally anxious for the visitor to depart. A retired Mountie tells of visiting a woodcutter two years in a row and of the woodcutter being surprised: "Why, you were here just last year. Anything wrong?" The Mountie succinctly summed up his relationship with them and other solitary people: "If they were sick, we took them to town; if they were dead, we buried them."

Most stayed along the river as long as their health and age permitted. They became attached to their horse and the three or four sled dogs. They had their cabins to take care of, sometimes a short trapline to run, always chores to do and the wood to cut. The popular image of men being trapped inside a cabin for months on end does not reflect the conditions

39

accurately. They stayed inside only when it was severely cold, when the thermometer dropped to 60 degrees below or lower. Above that, it is easier to keep warm than most Outsiders realize.

When the woodcutters did become too old to work, or too ill, usually they were taken to the Sisters of St. Ann's hospital and nursing home in Dawson City to live out the rest of their lives. Few returned to their place of birth and most of the earlier woodcutters were prospectors who failed to find gold, and for various reasons—embarrassment among them—chose to remain in the Yukon. More than one elderly woodcutter decided to make a last trip back to see his family, got as far south as Skagway, then retraced his route to the wilderness to die among those who understood his adopted way of life.

The life of telegraph operators was equally lonely, often more so since some were stationed deep in the wilderness of northern British Columbia where they could expect visitors no more often than once a year, when supplies were brought in to them by pack train. The line branched off the main Canadian trunk at Ashcroft and headed north through the absolute wilderness to the shore of Lake Atlin, skirted it and Tagish and Marsh lakes, followed the Yukon River through Whitehorse, Upper and Lower Laberge and Fort Selkirk, and continued into Dawson City, the original territorial capital.

The operators lived at roughly 50-mile intervals and were responsible for the line between them and the next station. Infrequently two men were assigned to a station, usually those a longer distance from the next; more often it was a solitary post. The occupation was not without its humor and drama. They were in constant communication with each other and there seemed to be the inevitable practical joker stationed somewhere along the system always. One prankster waited until the coldest night of the winter, then tapped out a message for all to look at the eclipse of the moon. For nearly a thousand miles operators crawled out of bed and into their layers of clothing and went outside to see a perfectly normal moon.

Sometimes operators became seriously ill, broke a limb or even accidentally shot themselves, and the other operators would stay by their telegraph key to follow subsequent events and cheer up the victim by sending out lonely, electrical impulses across the wilderness until help arrived. But most of the time it was simply lonely work. They made frequent patrols along the line to keep it clear, and reported in with a portable key they carried in their pack. Like the woodcutters, some kept dogs as much for pets as work animals, but food was a problem for those not on or near a large river. Since it was a specialized occupation, trips Outside for holidays, or vacations, were sparse, and it was not unusual for men to be confined to their post for two or three years at a stretch without more than the annual visit from the supply train.

The woodcutters' jobs were lost when the timber supply was so depleted that the steamboats converted to oil for fuel, and the telegraph operators were replaced by microwave towers atop mountains throughout Western Canada.

Today, cabin fever is more likely to take the form of "housewife's syndrome," due largely to the urbanization of the Yukon. When the syndrome occurred in the Canadian prairies, the first major defense against it was taken by companies that owned the grain elevators strung across the prairies beside railroad spurs. Married men were hired to operate the elevators, and, while they were away from the house filling freight cars or emptying wagons and trucks, their wives were confined to the house, often with small children and the sound of wind blowing eternally through the telegraph wires and around the corners of the house. There were many cases of women becoming depressed and a few cases of suicide or murder or both. The companies partially solved the problem by installing good radios in the houses, and phonographs with a wide selection of records. The advent of television helped considerably, and many women in the Yukon today keep the television set on all day as an antidote for the vast silence or the threatening sound of the winter wind.

Government psychiatrists working in the North have drawn up a composite of a potential cabin-fever victim, noting that today it is almost exclusively a woman's condition. The victim would be married and have small children, and she would not be working. She would have been born and reared in the Canadian provinces ("Outside"), because all emigrants go through a period of isolation on arrival in Canada and would be accustomed to stress before moving north. She would have no family or close friends in the new town, and her husband would be working long hours away from home, absorbed in his new job and have little time for his family. And, last, she probably didn't want to move to the North in the first place. Most women still follow rather than lead their husbands to the rims of society. The antidote for them, as it always has been for everyone, is to get busy; meet people; find a part-time job. Churches and social clubs have been encouraged to seek out newcomers and put them at ease in their new surroundings.

Contrary to the usual conception of the Yukon River and its headwaters, there are only a few people living in isolation today. Yukoners with a few winters' experience need little encouragement to find something in or near town to occupy themselves, and it is a rarity to find someone who doesn't make several trips to town each year, or move to town and forget about the romance of the North suggested by the works of Robert Service. Those who cling to a controlled solitude on the edge of civilization, those who accept society on their own terms, are numbered at less than a score in the whole Yukon drainage to the Alaska border. While those few by necessity live on major waterways for transportation and can be assured some visitors during the brief summer, they can also be virtually guaranteed privacy from October until May.

For more than a decade Reg Brooks, his wife and their youngest son have lived on Grahame Inlet under these conditions. We were anxious to meet them because they, unlike other families we knew along the river, seldom went to town and were discussed by other Northerners with a combination of respect and awe. There are others, of course, who speak of the Brookses and other solitary families as having lived in the wilderness so long that they have become "bushed," which apparently is akin to stir-crazy or odd, as some elderly Southern ladies who spend their declining years behind drawn shades have been called. We learned to dismiss such indictments as a symptom of the Yukon's urbanization and the inevitable contempt for nonconformity that follows population density.

To visit the Brookses we first had to run the Atlin River that drains the lake into Grahame Inlet. When we rented the canoe from Paul Lucier in Whitehorse, he stipulated that we hire a guide for the Atlin River and suggested we contact Stefan Shearer in Atlin, a "Yank" like us, and Paul pronounced his name STEF-an. When I found Stefan by following directions cheerfully given by children playing in a street, he corrected the pronounciation to ste-FAWN. When he came to the door of his small, tidy cabin, he was wearing a bright blue warmup suit over his short, wiry frame. We stood chatting a moment and I commented on the firewood stacked 4 or 5 feet high all around his yard like a fence. He replied that he received a great deal of enjoyment from contemplating the patterns created by the wood and the play of light and shadow upon it. I remembered that Carol Florence had said something similar, about the light hitting the side of the *Tarahane* and changing colors, and of how many different colors the sunsets made the snow on the Coast Range.

We agreed on a price and Stefan said he would meet us at the lake shore at one o'clock sharp. He arrived at 2:10 sharp, wearing baggy wool Malone pants, wool shirt and cap, and carrying a small knapsack with a sleeping bag. As he was introduced to the children, he accorded them the same courtesy he did my wife, and they brightened visibly at the attention and whispered pleas to ride with him in his small canoe powered by a tiny outboard.

We followed him slowly across the lake to the northwest, wallowing in the deep troughs and huddled beneath our ponchos and rain gear against the wind and occasional stings of cold spray. Earlier in the day the lake had been covered by fluffy clouds, but while we waited for Stefan they bunched together into a solid gray mass that obscured the top of Atlin Mountain. Now it was raining lightly and getting quite dark, although the day had at least eight hours of light remaining.

We rounded the point of an island and threaded among some smaller ones and into Scotia Bay. We tied up at the decrepit dock where the narrow-gauge railroad had ended and steamboat transportation began. The years and vandals had taken their toll on the dock and small cabin, and it was impossible to find a sheltered place to stand out of the rain and wind.

The Atlin River begins only a few feet south of the dock and a large, smooth, watermarked rock almost evenly divides its birthplace. The whitewater begins almost immediately, low riffles at first that grow into foam toward the first curve. Stefan took his canoe into the stream to test its strength, occasionally peering over the side to check the depth. Sometimes he held the canoe stationary against the current, then let it drift backward. While he was thus occupied, the children amused themselves by skipping back and forth on the railroad ties and tried to worry us by hiding in the brush until giggles betrayed them. Stefan pulled out of the river and beached his canoe, then repeated the process with the freighter. We helped him conceal his canoe and motor in the brush, and we were ready to run the river.

Although the Atlin is only 2 miles long, it drops more than 50 feet and has several sharp bends and rocks that create standing waves and backwashes. Without realizing it, we had selected the safest time to run it, in late June before the heavy runoff began. Later in the summer the rock at the entrance would be almost submerged and the river would be a maze of standing waves. One curve is so narrow that Stefan said the water stands on its edge during most of August. He wasn't worried about these problems now, only that the water was so shallow he might ding the prop or snap the shear pin. A 22-foot freighter canoe that weighs more than five hundred pounds, plus another thousand pounds of people and gear, is not an easy craft to paddle. He said our only danger would be losing power and turning broadside to the current and hitting a rock. Everyone wore flotation gear, but Stefan told us that one of the last men to drown in the river had worn a proper life jacket, too.

He stationed me in the bow with a paddle and we entered the river. Absolutely nothing happened. As the children had said a year earlier after running Five Finger Rapids on the Yukon River: "Is that all? Boring!"

We cruised smoothly down the crooked river past a beaver dam and over the low rapids with Stefan keeping just enough power on for steerage. The river widened slightly as it entered Grahame Inlet, and we swung back around to the north past an island to land at the abandoned railroad station of Taku.

Stefan had planned to walk back to Lake Atlin on the old railroad right-of-way, but we asked him to stay overnight with us and share the moose and caribou steaks the Florences had given us that morning. Since his wife was away overnight, Stefan agreed, and he took the children on a fishing expedition to the river mouth while we set up camp.

That evening he told us his wife was a native of France and he, of Southern California. Both were avid outdoors people and they migrated to Atlin for its solitude and great alpine skiing. Each summer they cached food in several places back in the bush, then ate it the following winter on cross-country skiing trips. They had made several trips across the icecap to the Alaska coast, sometimes taking a small group of skiers with them.

He said they could live nicely on $2,000 a year and were vegetarians the first year in Atlin. But resisting the sight of those gorgeous moose steaks and roasts was beyond their willpower. The second autumn, Stefan joined other men in Atlin, shouldered a rifle and shot a moose. He said a moose was worth $500 in meat, but that he and his wife, Françoise, still subsist mainly on vegetables and health food, which they import in bulk orders and sell to other people in the area.

He caught three grayling, which he cleaned for breakfast and hung high in a tree. Then he further cemented his friendship with the children by popping the fish eyes down his throat with great relish. They were astonished, and even the bravest of the four could not bring herself to try what Stefan said was a great delicacy.

We preferred our fish a bit fresher and placed ours in a Ziploc plastic bag in the lake near the tents, weighted down with rocks. That night we heard a determined rattling and shined the flashlight around until we found two beady, steady eyes glaring back at us from the area of our fish. A weasel had found our breakfast. We went back to bed without bothering him; he had earned the fish.

It always surprised us to explore the ghost towns and

find furniture, clothing, stoves and utensils still in the cabins and, in the case of Taku, tools in the shops. But Taku is too close to Atlin, and the cabins had been ravaged by vandals rather than thieves. Bullet holes decorated the few windows still intact. Furniture was slashed into rubbish and some pieces had been broken up for firewood.

Each of the four or five buildings at Taku still had usable items in it that had been there since the mid-1950s when the *Little Duchess* was loaded onto a barge and towed to Carcross by the *Tutshi,* both en route to museum status. Three flatcars had been left behind, so small that they looked custom built for a large model railroad rather than a small working railroad. They were hooked together at the end of the dock that first swayed in the middle, then listed toward the lake as if undecided whether to fall in on itself or shrug the flatcars off into the cold water.

Of all the headwater lakes, Grahame Inlet is perhaps the least interesting visually, while one of the safest for small boats. No tall mountains are reflected on it, no rocks or clusters of islands give visual relief. Instead, it bears a remarkable resemblance to the artificial lakes that can be found throughout North America behind hydroelectric dams. It is something of an interlude between the vast Atlin and the fjordlike Taku Arm with the Florence Range climbing directly out of it to spires more than 7,000 feet high.

We left Stefan at Taku and cruised down the narrow inlet toward the Brookses' place. Joe Florence had told them we were coming, and when we pulled up at their sturdy pier, Reg and his son, Jim, came out to help us tie up and unload. Brooks is a tall, broad man with short gray hair and an easy stride that can cover many miles without rest. He led us to the house where he said his wife would soon have lunch for us. She met us at the door, a small, slender woman with glasses and a warm, friendly smile. To our delight they served coffee rather than tea, and we chatted in the warm cabin while she finished cooking on the big wood stove that kept the cabin toasty against the chilly wind that occasionally gusted through the open front door.

The cabin was large with a walled sleeping room in a

back corner. The log walls were devoid of homey decorations, other than a tanned wolf skin stretched across one wall. Kerosene lanterns, traps, tools, snowshoes, rifles and other wilderness paraphernalia were hung at random and somehow looked more attractive than paintings and antiques. Stacked around the stove and kitchen area were several boxes of canned food; there were no cupboards or drawers for storage, and it was obvious the Brookses lived out of the boxes like migratory workers.

"We use this place only as summer quarters," Brooks explained. "During the winter months we live like nomads, running the traplines from cabin to cabin we have back in the bush."

"I'm their skinner," Mrs. Brooks said with a laugh.

They had a dog team tied to individual houses on the lake shore and assured us they were perfectly safe for the children.

"We treat them like pets," Brooks said. "When we're on the trapline, I walk ahead and lead them, and break trail for them. We don't ride in the sled—most of the country is too rough for that anyway. I don't believe in abusing animals to make them work."

Reg's father was a mining engineer and managed the Engineer Gold Mine a few miles away on Taku Arm when it was operating. He apparently felt more at ease in the wilderness than the Outside and was one of the few miners to stake out a land claim in the area and live on it. When the mine closed, he moved to Vancouver, where Reg and his family lived for several years. They were never content in the city, and when Reg's father was quite old he asked to be taken back to the cabin on Grahame Inlet for the last time. The whole family made a summer of it, and when fall came Reg had decided to move back to the wilderness to stay. Their oldest son joined the Navy, but Jim, then ten or eleven, went with them and completed his schooling by correspondence.

"Schooling is a big problem with couples living in the bush," Brooks said. "They're usually fine for a few years when they're alone or the children are small. But when they're school age, few parents make them keep up with their studies. Then the school authorities come and tell them they will either have to keep up with the courses or the kids must be taken to town."

It was no problem with Jim. His specialty is geology, and the Brookses' small library leans heavily into that field with a small but solid selection of texts on the subject, which Jim has virtually memorized. His education is furthered nearly every summer when groups of graduate students in geology make field trips to the area and Jim badgers them and the professor for information which he soaks up like moss does rain.

They go to town twice a year: in the spring to Carcross by boat to catch the train to Whitehorse and buy a year's supply of food while delivering their pelts; and to Atlin each Christmas, weather and lake ice permitting. They stay with a family friend in Atlin, an elderly bachelor who each visit must show them how to kill a bear barehanded. He demonstrates the fatal headhold on his dog, and Jim said that each time the subject comes up, the dog starts getting extremely agitated. When the old man calls him over for the demonstration, he tucks his tail in and heads for the door. "Can't understand what gets into that dog," the old man says, genuinely puzzled.

When they are unable to make the Atlin trip, it is because the weather is very bad or the lake ice isn't thick enough. Lake Atlin's size often keeps the ice unsafe during mild winters, and Brooks is not an impatient or daring man. Usually the Mounties will bring their Christmas mail in a helicopter, stop long enough for a cup of tea, then continue their rounds to others living away from town.

At various times throughout the day the Brookses performed a ritual we were to see repeated in every home in remote areas. They settled around the table and turned on the battery-powered radio to listen to the news. The regional news seems of less interest to them than the national, which often was about evenly divided between Canadian and U.S. reports. Like most Canadians, they show a remarkable knowledge of and concern for U.S. matters, yet do not blame us as individuals for our nation's ills anymore than they would blame each other for Canada's problems.

The Brookses listened carefully to the weather report, as people do everywhere, and discarded most of it as useless for anyone living so near the weather-making icecap. Brooks insists you can't depend on forecasts at all; you just take what it gives and accept it.

"You always give yourself lots of time to travel up here," Brooks says, "and you don't force your luck. If you're out in a boat and it starts blowing, you pull in to shore and sit it out. If it turns bad in the winter, you hole up until it passes. You always travel prepared for the worst."

He said that when they're trapping and a sudden warm spell comes, they usually stay out of the bush until it gets cold again. "If a bear's den gets flooded, he's going to come out very hungry, very mad, and very unpredictable. I don't care to be there. Spring is another bad time for the same reason; until the bears get some food in them, they can be pretty cantankerous."

Several times during the long conversation and leisurely lunch of whitefish, potatoes and homemade bread, Brooks repeated his cardinal rules of the bush: "You live with the land up here. Don't force it."

We listened but didn't hear. We were traveling on a set schedule that called for us to camp on Taku Arm that night. In spite of the rain that was turning into a gray downpour, we were determined to contine. Reg said nothing, observing that northern courtesy of living and letting live, and stood in the rain and watched us depart. We went less than a quarter of a mile before most of us were shivering uncontrollably and water was sloshing in the bottom of the boat. With no discussion necessary, we executed a U-turn and returned, the lesson he'd been pounding into us learned at last.

To supplement their income, the Brookses have built three or four cozy log cabins back of their cabin, each with its own screen of trees, and rent them to the occasional visitor or fishing group. Without a trace of I-told-you-so commentary, Reg and Jim helped us unload the canoe and lug our duffel bags to one of the cabins. Within five minutes the wood stove had us thawed out. The cabin was so new that the peeled logs hadn't cured yet and the aroma of pitch and newly cut wood gave it a sweet, clean smell. It was equipped with four bunks, the stove, one or two old chairs and a shelf near the door for two washbasins. On a lower shelf we found some rudimentary cooking

49

and eating utensils and a diagram that told us how to filet fish with a minimum of cutting. Out behind the cabin was a pit for dishwater and garbage, which Brooks covered with dirt frequently to keep bears uninterested.

After the children were bedded down, we blew out the kerosene lamp and went back to visit the Brookses. In our ignorance of the North, we were vaguely disappointed in them. We had expected someone out of a Jack London yarn or a Robert Service poem. Instead, we were visiting three very friendly low-keyed and self-sufficient people. They were not impressed with themselves for living in a manner no longer necessary and one that appealed to many young people at the time. They were not defensive about their life, nor were they apologetic. We saw in them a contentment we were to see in other families from time to time, a serenity we have seen only occasionally among our farmer friends, who are equally at peace with their surroundings.

The Brookses did not recommend their life for others, for they knew from past experience that few couples could make the move successfully from the city to the wilderness. The prospect of going to the outhouse when the temperature hangs at 40 degrees below is enough to make sure most of us only dream of the wilderness way of life. But the Brookses and a handful of other people are uniquely equipped for such a life, and one of the major qualifications is emotional stability. Without it the isolation can turn one's thoughts inward and contort the personality. Rather than enjoying our surroundings, as the Brookses do, most of us have neuroses that tend to emerge and blossom like parasitic moss on a tree. There are some in the North who have become cantankerous over the years, and their friends, while sympathetic, give them a wide berth. It is an embarrassing and frightening thing to watch a personality deteriorate. Those who understand this phenonemon do not joke about it among themselves. They are more likely to limit their commentary to an eloquent, sad shake of the head.

Far down the river from the Brookses, less than fifty miles from Dawson City, we read the autobiography of such a case in an old woodcutters' camp we found that apparently had not been visited since the last occupant was taken away on a steamboat. The cabin and barn had long since caved in, and neither could be seen from the river. Wild roses almost covered the buildings, and tall grass and fireweed grew in profusion on what little remained of the cabin's sod roof.

We found a plank ramp that was used to push wheelbarrows of wood onto the steamboats, and we appropriated it for a similar use. After dinner we began the rather sad exercise of exploring the area. The last inhabitant had left behind his lantern, a few clothes, his ax and saws, parts of harness and a small library of religious and communist literature. The emphasis was on the former. The books were in remarkably good condition and had been protected from the weather by part of the roof that had caved in on top of them. They ran to the fundamental theology and were illustrated with vivid paintings in greens and reds showing Lucifer being kicked out of Heaven, then his fiendish emergence as the leader of Hell. One picture showed Lucifer and his cronies posing in Hell, each with the demented look of a satyr. The text—what little we read, since it was a dark and gloomy campsite—was of the type that tells us what a miserable species we are and that our nature is so gross that there is only a tiny particle of hope for our souls. It made for depressing reading and we soon put it back where we found it, but wrapped in a plastic bread wrapper to protect it from decay. It was not the kind of book one treats casually, nor was it the kind one would take away from its resting place.

Whatever that woodcutter's personal history, he succeeded in casting a pall over camp that night, and we talked about him around the campfire, wondering about the mental state of a man who would collect such literature. We tried to imagine what his life must have been like during the long winter with his horse and two or three dogs for companionship while he read those books that told him his species was no good, and the communist pamphlets that told him the governments of the Western Hemisphere were no better. It was impossible to imagine him a jovial man, and when the steamboats stopped for wood he probably helped load them silently, then turned back toward his cabin, one of the few men on the whole river who refused to wave good-bye to the crew and passengers; a solitary man at ease in the wilderness but not in this world.

I told an old-timer about the camp and our theory of the man's personality, and he gave that eloquent, sad shake of the head and said it sounded like one of the poor souls the Mounties had to move off the river and out of the North from time to time. The simple, basic life of wilderness living seems to amplify both faults and virtues, strengths and weaknesses.

The Brookses made our last four days on the lake trip from Atlin to Whitehorse anticlimactic. We were caught in the middle of Taku Arm by a storm with rain and wind so cold that two of the children cried from the pain. We also sat out a spectacular electrical storm that came up on us after a hot, still day. We saw postcard waterfalls and caught Arctic grayling with ease where small streams entered the lake. We camped on a tiny, rocky island with the Florence Range climbing vertically out of the lake a few feet away to catch the first light of morning. We had a whole day of absolutely calm weather with the lake reflecting the mountains and clouds perfectly, and we amused ourselves by watching the canoe's wake curves bend and distort the reflections and felt mildly guilty for disturbing such peaceful and beautiful scenes.

But our meeting with the Brookses robbed us of the sense of discovery we felt on the first half of the trip. We knew they had been over these lakes repeatedly for more than a decade and that they had been more uncomfortable and in more dangerous situations. They had seen the lakes at the peak of their seasonal beauty; in the fall when the colors change rapidly, in the winter when they are white and tinted blue where the ice is thin and in the spring when the snow is gone but the ice is still there and they are waiting for it to clear so they can go to town.

We didn't object to sharing those beauties and discomforts. But it seemed we had trespassed on their realm of experience, and they had been too gracious to mention it.

Whitehorse

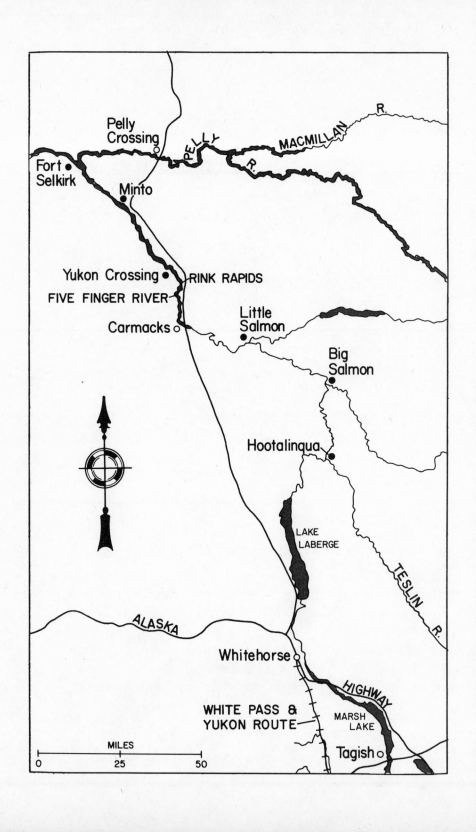

The violence and drama and beauty of birth are totally absent at the Yukon River's birthplace on Marsh Lake. It is as though the lakes wear themselves out the farther north they stretch, then in fatigue and defeat, become a river. The alpine beauty of Taku Arm and Tagish Lake flattens and turns gray. The limestone and granite mountains, bald of timber, make Marsh a totally unremarkable lake; shallow with the smoothed-down hills wandering aimlessly back into the wilderness. To complete the anticlimax of the headwaters, the Alaska Highway runs the length of Marsh and an almost permanent ribbon of dust hangs on the eastern shore, coating the trees and brush from the gravel highway to the lake. There is no sense of wilderness here, nor is there again for nearly a hundred miles until beyond Lake Laberge.

Some 90 percent of the Yukon Territory's population is gathered within fifty miles of the 60th Parallel: Carcross, Tagish and the north end of Marsh Lake and Whitehorse. Summer homes with boat docks are clustered on the north end of Marsh Lake with a promise of more to come, since the federal government has freed additional land for cabins. The lake is warmer than the others because it is shallow, and droning speedboats pulling waterskiers are a permanent fixture on long summer days.

While the river begins ignominiously, after several days of traveling on slack water we were excited at the prospect of letting the water itself provide part of the power. There would be no more twitches of guilt for disturbing the flat, reflective water, nor would there be the discomfort of bucking heavy seas. The current even promised a measure of safety if we capsized; at least we could use it to be swept ashore rather than swimming in frigid water that leaches off body heat.

The river's first monument to civilization appears just downstream from the Alaska Highway bridge, a dam built by the White Pass & Yukon Route during the steamboat era. It was erected so that each spring when the river ice cleared, but Lake Laberge was still icelocked, the floodgates could be opened to send a cascade of water down through Miles Canyon, over the rapids at Whitehorse, past the waiting paddlewheelers and into the broad 30-mile-long lake to flush out the ice. Today it is used as a regulatory and flood control dam, but it is doubtful anyone would miss it should it collapse.

Boaters following the river go through a small lock that must be operated by the boaters themselves and is large enough for a medium-sized yacht, then continue on down the river past the tilted sweepers hanging drunkenly out over the river and grassy banks where moose sometimes come down to graze and drink.

The river above Whitehorse had perhaps two dozen steamboats on it over the years, all headed downstream, none of which ever saw this part of the river again. There were two distinct steamboat routes; the lake system described earlier that ran south from Carcross and the river system that ran from Whitehorse north. The train was the connecting link. Once a lake boat went to Whitehorse, it never returned. After it navigated Miles Canyon and the rapids, it could never go back up the crevice of the canyon.

The river runs normally enough, sweeping around bend after bend, until it reaches Miles Canyon, where for about a hundred yards it is compressed into a gap between two sheer walls of basalt less than 50 feet wide. Until the hydroelectric dam was built at Whitehorse, the river poured through the crevice full force with vicious crosscurrents and a 3-foot crest in the center that ripped and roiled and foamed and dashed boats piloted by the uninitiated against the cliffs. The canyon ends abruptly and at either side of the downstream opening were whirlpools that could and did swallow rowboats and rafts.

Those who successfully ran the canyon still had to face the two sets of rapids downstream, Squaw and White Horse, the latter named for the white standing waves that resembled horses' manes. Squaw Rapids had large rocks standing above the water's surface that, sirenlike, seemed to beckon boats to them.

During the insanity of the gold rush, the hikers who became boaters at Lake Bennett were stopped by Miles Canyon and the rapids. Of those who shot them, only a fraction emerged at the downstream end with boat, body, and baggage intact. The more cautious lined their boats down and packed their gear over a 5-mile portage. Since they were in a race to the goldfields, many cast off and took their chances.

The Mounties, who on the passes had protected the boaters from the avarice of each other and their own stupidity, reentered the stampede at Miles Canyon. The commanding officer, an incredibly tough and wise man named Samuel Steele, decreed that no women and children would ride boats through the soaked Hades, and that only pilots endorsed by himself could take boats through. He imposed a fine for the disobedient so there could be no question that he was serious. (For years the legend persisted that Jack London earned a small fortune working as a pilot through Miles Canyon, and a sign to that effect was placed at a viewpoint overlooking the canyon. But it later was painted over when a historian discovered that, while London ran the rapids, he kept going without stopping.)

While Steele was attempting to impose order on a process that is inherently disorderly, a man named Norman Macaulay set about making his fortune in the transportation business. He built a railway-tramway from above the canyon at Canyon City (let three people camp somewhere in a gold rush and it will become a city) around the bad water on the east side of the river to a site across from where Whitehorse now stands. Macaulay put crude horse-drawn carts on the rails and began hauling stampeders' gear—sometimes the boats too—around to good water again. In a short time he became a wealthy man and was one of those few who retired to the Outside with his cash intact.

Today Miles Canyon can still give boaters a thrill. It still flows through the canyon and has a trace of its strength left, but it is an old, toothless lion.

Geography, rather than an unethical real estate developer, created Whitehorse. Upriver steamboat navigation stopped there, and so did the White Pass & Yukon Route tracks from Skagway. It was a baggage and passenger terminal that for decades pretended to be nothing else. So far as most northerners were concerned, that was sufficient; the town had no other reason to exist and no known reason to grow. It had nothing of interest to the tourist industry, no natural beauty, and little history other than Miles Canyon. It sat huddled in an unattractive valley with soil of volcanic ash that would hardly grow weeds. It was simply a way station en route to Dawson City.

One could blame the Japanese for its growth to become the Yukon's major city. When World War II broke out and the Japanese invaded Alaska's Aleutian Islands, the United States became intensely interested in the north, which earlier had been dismissed as Seward's Folly and General Billy Mitchell's pipe dream. Supplies had to be moved in and the government, with Canada's blessing, decided to build a highway from Dawson Creek, in northwest British Columbia, to Anchorage.

Canadians in British Columbia and the Yukon still shake their heads in amazement at the waste involved in the highway construction, although it was completed in record time. And there are stories of Yukoners who somehow imported cars and trucks where there were no roads before, using the military's Alaska Highway as their own private thoroughfares. Others went around to abandoned equipment caches and put together vehicles, often weird hybrids, and drove them home.

But the highway was sent through Whitehorse to connect with the railroad and river and, of equal strategic importance, the oil pipeline that for a short time ran from Norman Wells on the Mackenzie River in the Northwest Territories to Whitehorse.

Suddenly the transfer station became a boom town. The military built an airfield on a hill above town that was used as a refueling station for planes en route to Alaska or Russia on the lend-lease program. When the war ended and the Alaska Highway was opened to civilian traffic, Whitehorse gradually replaced Dawson City as the destination for business, and the latter began its inevitable decline. It did not require the services of a prophet or a study group to foresee the time when upstart Whitehorse would be trying to move the territorial capital more than 300 miles south to the crossroads of commerce.

Surrounded by low, gray, bald mountains, Whitehorse resembles a small western town such as those one can find in eastern Colorado, southern Wyoming, or Kansas. It has all the requirements for a small town—an Arctic Circle drive-in, a Colonel Sanders fried chicken emporium, low-profile and pre-fabricated office buildings designed by service-station architects, a mobile home park on the outskirts, a cluster of duplex frame military housing now constituting a neighborhood, and streets that are dusty in the summer and icy in the winter.

Traffic during the summer months is constant and loud on the main streets, although the town has only about 12,000 residents. The large and recent crop of motels could be borrowed from any part of the continent, and the town is almost totally lacking in any feature to establish it as subarctic. It is as though a Middle American town were placed on trailers and hauled north, then set down in the most unlikely townsite anyone could find. One has to read bank signs to recognize Whitehorse as Canadian.

The only structures that might inform the visitor he was anywhere other than on the eastern slopes of the Rocky Mountains are a three-story log cabin apartment building and the museum piece, the paddlewheeler *Klondike*. But the old steamboat is on the edge of town rather than its center and it could have been built by Walt Disney's staff for a northern Disneyland.

Across the river is a subdivision called Riverdale, composed of overpriced homes jammed at what seems only arm's length apart and looking more native to Southern California than the North. Only the long summer days and the frigid, dark nights of winter attest to the latitude. The pioneer culture has been swept up, demolished, burned, or shunted aside to crumble and fall of its own weight and age. Whitehorse has no time for the luxuries of the past; it is too busy a-building. Perhaps in a few decades, after all traces of the past have been erased and all the pioneers are dead, the town will follow the example of other frontiers and frantically recapture as much of its past as possible.

What record of its past still exists is found only in the memories of those who lived there before World War II and in photograph collections housed in the territorial archives. The old-timers of the Yukon become increasingly bitter about this abhorrence for things past, yet admit there is nothing unusual about it. Canada, more than the United States, is a land of recent immigrants, and the frontier, like an immigrant family, must go through at least three generations before the past becomes important again and the languages and customs of the elders that were intentionally forgotten (and often denied) are relearned with a vengeance. The Yukon frontier is in its second generation. The grandchildren of the old stampeders of seventy-five years ago will soon start demanding restoration and preservation projects.

One of the most certain indications that the frontier is closed occurs when towns begin festivals to honor their past and make money off tourists in the process. (Whoever heard of a festival that wasn't supposed to make money?) In Whitehorse it is the Sourdough Rendezvous held at the end of each February and advertised as a northern Mardi Gras, a sure cure for cabin fever. Charter flights from Vancouver and Edmonton drop hundreds of party-goers in town for the weekend, and enterprising travel agents have found that northerners will even go elsewhere in the North during the depths of winter. So other charter flights originate in Yellowknife, Northwest Territories, often with civil servants from far away coming to Whitehorse to tell civil servants there that their town is ugly.

Townspeople dress in period costumes and women tend toward dancehall-style short skirts; men usually choose dandy gamblers' uniforms. All businesses require their staff to dress for the event, and one bank even stages a robbery each Rendezvous.

The locals stay outside more and either watch or participate in the endless round of sled dog races—sled dogs have become as popular in the North as horses in the West now that they seldom are used. People stand for hours on the bank of the frozen Yukon River watching the teams and drivers disappear around a bend in the river—and nearly an hour later come back upriver slowly, painfully to the finish line.

Snowmobile races are almost equally popular, and middle-aged men roar through the starting area, serious as little boys pretending they are General Patton, tearing around in circles and getting as close to bystanders as they can to see who will jump, always with that stern, serious and totally incongruous expression on their faces. Bystanders soon learn that if they ignore them and yield not an inch, the drivers will leave them alone. And it probably ruins the snowmobilers' entire day.

Every year there are some visitors, usually from Vancouver or Edmonton, who arrive in Whitehorse and vow they are going to neither sleep nor leave their room until it is time to catch a plane back home—not because they dread the cold, but because they plan to have a permanent party. One year it was the vice-president of a winery in British Columbia who made the vow. He loaded the plane with dozens of cases of wine and champagne, passed it out freely during the two-and-a-half-hour flight to Whitehorse, headed directly to his motel room after insisting everyone come whenever they wanted to and set up shop for the long weekend. He was accompanied by a rather long, elegant blonde who spent an inordinate amount of time clad only in a beach towel while reclining on the bed like a superrealistic, perhaps inflatable art object. The party went on and on, and when it got loud, the management called the room several times to ask them to be quiet. Weary of the telephone, the winery officer stood on the bed beside the blonde, punched a hole in the ceiling with his fist and put the phone up there for the rest of the weekend.

The townspeople work as hard at fun as the visitors, and the YWCA in Whitehorse transforms its lower floor and recreation room into a casino for the weekend. An employee sits at the front desk, ostensibly to keep registered guests and transient guests separated; but, either by intent or lack of concern, the task is not pursued with vigor.

As the weekend draws to a close, more and more visitors drive the 20 miles out to Takhini Hot Springs Resort where, for a nominal sum, they can rent a swim suit and towel and swim in the steaming outdoor pool while the air temperature is below zero. The braver ones dash out of the pool and roll in the snow until they turn blue and hypothermia sets in. It delights bystanders to watch the chameleon changes of the swimmers' bodies: white on entering the pool, pink after a few minutes in the hot water, white again when they hit the snow, and blue when they dive back into the pool again.

Little work is accomplished the day after the Rendezvous ends as people stay home to nurse gigantic hangovers or catch up on sleep. Charter flights away from Whitehorse are notable for their stillness.

For the Yukoners, the Rendezvous means that spring isn't far away and that the days will get increasingly longer. Two months of cold weather remain, and the lakes and river will be free of ice in about three months. They know they can begin thinking of winter in the past tense while bragging about their devastating hangovers. The tourist industry counts its money, repairs the damage and waits for the next onslaught of visitors in the summer, most of whom will be elderly people on package tours. They will be in Whitehorse only long enough for a few meals, a tour that takes about an hour, a night in a hotel; and then they're gone forever, faceless wallets, credit cards and coupon books.

In spite of its increasing income, tourism will remain low on the governmental priority scale for decades to come. To most people, the Yukon will always be synonymous with mining. Gold created it, and other minerals since discovered govern it today. As the provincial governments impose higher taxes on mining and discoveries, the high-risk investors will keep moving north. Already backpackers are complaining that nowhere in the wilderness is one immune to the sound of helicopters overhead, and that abandoned prospecting camps with gasoline drums, plastic bottles and other garbage are becoming commonplace.

There is virtually no wilderness or conservation ethic at work in Whitehorse. Conversations in bars and hotel lobbies are bluntly and without guilt directed toward exploitation of the mineral resources. Geologists and prospectors believe the real mining boom is yet to come. Exploration is one of the major sources of revenue to the territory, and there are helicopter charter firms whose entire, and substantial, income is from hauling geologists in and out of the bush in search of minerals and oil.

Consequently, the rumors of big strikes are rampant throughout the year, particularly during the summer months when capitalists from North America, Europe, Japan and Hong Kong filter into town, then leave early some morning in a helicopter to look over promising claims. On almost any given August day hotel owners can say they've had investors from Switzerland, Los Angeles or Vancouver staying overnight, and in the three or four good restaurants in Whitehorse men can be seen leaning forward and speaking in low tones.

The greatest success story of them all is the Anvil Mine, the largest of six mines operating in the territory. The Anvil is about 230 miles northeast of Whitehorse near Ross River, and it went into production in 1969. Its known deposits of silver, lead and zinc are $3 billion, and ore trucks run on the average of one every 17 minutes between Ross River and the railroad at Whitehorse. Its production and deposits dwarf the other mines: Cassiar (asbestos), Keno Hill (silver, lead, zinc and cadmium), Quill Creek (nickel and copper), Whitehorse (copper) and the small coal mine, Tantalus Butte, near Carmacks.

Al Kulan, the Anvil discoverer, is a legendary character in the Yukon, in part because he seldom bothers to deny or confirm the tales that are told about him. His net worth is known only by the government, his accountant and his partners, but he has said he can "lose half a million and not be hurt."

He began as another summer-only prospector with a family to support and debts to pay off each winter. But he adhered to the basic rules of prospecting: a fresh, open approach to everything, and an ability to see something that does not belong. Then he added his own rule: he worked only a small area, rather than tearing all over the Yukon in a helicopter. He says he knows some prospectors who are so busy looking for outcroppings of ore that they never get out of a helicopter long enough to see one.

Unlike the more usual prospector—the one who either

blows his money when he makes a discovery or is so broke to begin with that he must sell below its value—Kulan has been as wise in money matters as he was in the search; he has his wealth and it is still growing. His single concession to sudden wealth was the purchase of a Rolls-Royce, which he drove back to Ross River over dusty, rough roads and used like a Jeep for several years. It was a source of amusement among Yukoners to see Kulan's elegant car with picks, shovels, axes and prospector friends in the back seat. Eventually he traded it for a more traditional car because repairs were so difficult. Besides, he said, "Rolls are overrated."

He still lives in Ross River, one of the few white men in the town, and comes to Whitehorse only occasionally, sometimes to badger other miners and prospectors into selling or donating rare specimens of minerals to the Yukon mineral museum he's building at Ross River. Typically, he says it is not a philanthropic urge; he plans to make some money on it while preserving unique and representative specimens in the area they're from. He continues prospecting, not because he wants more money but because that is the kind of work he does.

The exact story of the Anvil discovery is known only by Kulan and a handful of other people, and he does not discuss it freely. The most common version is that an Indian friend told Kulan about a strange outcropping of rock on a creek off the Pelly River. That tip led to the Anvil discovery, and Kulan gave the Indian some shares in the mine, which were lost in legal shufflings and poor management by the Indian himself. Then, a few years later, the Indian and two friends were killed in a head-on crash with an Anvil truck. To compound the irony, the Indian's name was Joe Ladue, and it was another Joe Ladue who spent thirteen or fourteen years in the Yukon, founded Dawson City when the Klondike discovery was made, then went Outside to die the same year of the big stampede.

Kulan looks and speaks more like a college geology teacher out on a consulting job than one's usual burro-and-beard image of a prospector. He is a small, trim man with gray, wavy hair and wears horn-rimmed glasses. When other prospectors and geologists are in town, Kulan can be found at a table in a bar listening more than talking, filing away bits and pieces of conversations for future use when he goes into the bush. Sometimes it doesn't work to his advantage, though.

"I was working with a couple of men on a deal once and whispered to the waitress to serve me only ginger ale," Kulan said. "Later I found out the other guys did the same thing."

He has definite opinions on how the Yukon should be governed ("I like the Chinese because their values haven't changed in a thousand years"), and when he disagrees with a policy he is likely to take direct action against it. For example, the Canadian government would not set up a community television antenna at Ross River because regulations limited them to towns in excess of 500 population. It wasn't illegal for CBC technicians to tell him how to build one, which they did. Kulan built his own. He installed it near Ross River and it worked perfectly—much to the government's chagrin, since most of theirs did not. Then, in a burst of generosity—and with some malice—he gave it to the government.

He believes, and hopes, that if the Yukon cannot develop an agricultural base, it will remain sparsely populated. He is content in Ross River and has turned down opportunities to purchase vacation property in warmer climates because he does not want to become encumbered with ownership. But his own success is a threat. The mine plans to build a smelter at Ross River, which he says would pollute the air and river. If it is built, he says he will leave.

The other, less fortunate, prospectors continue living with their hopes. Some who have reached their eightieth year are still as enthusiastic and hopeful as a child. "I know an old man here who lives completely in the future," Kulan said. "He's a delight and is always planning his next spring so he can go out and look again. The freedom of the work is the important thing."

A friend who lives in Whitehorse, but keeps an emotional distance from it, is fond of saying, "There's Whitehorse, then there's the Yukon. One bears no relationship to the other." As with all oversimplifications, it has its origin in truth. Whitehorse people appear to take their role as Yukoners much more seriously than those living in other towns or in the bush. They work at being Yukoners, and there is a stubborn determination to their fun not found in Dawson City, where humor tends to be spontaneous rather than forced.

Whitehorse, year after year, has the distinction of consuming more alcoholic beverages per capita than any other city in Canada. Taverns and bars are the social centers of town, and the drinking laws are so relaxed that one can drink while driving, drink while walking, drink while standing at the corner waiting for one of Whitehorse's two traffic lights to change. Yet, except for the proverbial drunken Indians, of which there are many, there are few staggering drunks seen in bars or on the streets. It is not good form to drink that much, and a premium is placed on holding one's liquor. The Indians who drink at the Whitehorse Inn (Moccasin Square Garden in local parlance) are excepted. Alcoholism remains their major problem.

There are men who will tell you in all honesty that they drink and smoke during the winter months when they're forced into town by the weather, but return to the bush in June to run their wilderness fishing camps or to prospect and never drink or smoke until summer ends again. But during the winter the alcoholic consumption goes up as the thermometer drops. It is simply what people do.

More than anyone else in the Yukon, Whitehorse residents use the ethics of Robert Service's poetry as a guideline for their life-styles—although Service certainly did not advocate drinking all winter. Service is what sets the Yukon apart in the world's consciousness from the rest of the North. He is the unofficial poet laureate of the Yukon, and his long ballads, ranging from the humorous to the pseudophilosophical, have attracted more people to the Yukon than any other stimulus. He described Yukoners the way Yukoners like to think of themselves. There are many who have never camped out all night away from town and still believe they are living the life that Service chronicled.

In most categories, the Yukon has less to offer than its neighbors Alaska and the Northwest Territories. It isn't as mountainous and dramatic as Alaska, nor so vast and varied as the Northwest Territories. There have been gold rushes for both its neighbors, and their history and adventure stories are equally interesting. But neither have had someone to tell them and the rest of the world that this place is separate, special. It is the Yukon, and the Klondike as told by Service. It is nature imitating doggerel.

Even the most harsh critic of poetry, those who think Rudyard Kipling was a skillful Edgar Guest, cannot help but be moved by lines from Service's rhythmic poems:

> There's a land where the mountains are nameless,
> And the rivers all run God knows where;
> There are lives that are erring and aimless,
> And deaths that hang just by a hair;
> There are hardships that nobody reckons;
> There are valleys unpeopled and still;
> There's a land—oh, it beckons and beckons,
> And I want to go back—and I will.

Service is a folk hero in the Yukon, and his books sell better than the Bible. The Mounties have sometimes complained that they find more unprepared wanderers headed up the Alaska Highway attracted to the Yukon by Service than any other cause. Even those Americans who do not know that the Yukon is in Canada, rather than a part of Alaska, still head north because they are under the spell of Robert Service, a mild, shy bank clerk whose major influence was Kipling.

Service didn't arrive in the Yukon until the gold rush was already a memory. He had wandered around most of North America after leaving his native Scotland and was in Central America when the gold rush ran its course. He became active in the Anglican Church in Whitehorse and lived in quarters provided by the bank behind the business office. The story is told that he wrote his first ballad, "The Shooting of Dan McGrew," while out for his daily stroll. The church was producing an evening of entertainment and had asked Service to give a poetry reading, as he often had done in the past. He had been writing verse off and on for several years but had never read any of it in public, nor had he submitted it for publication.

With the invitation in mind, Service began searching for

a replacement for the usual material—Kipling's "Gunga Din" or the old "Face on the Barroom Floor." While out on his evening stroll, he passed a saloon from which loud voices and jukebox music emitted, and the first line of a ballad came to him: "A bunch of the boys were whooping it up"

He kept walking and composing, working out a plot involving a love triangle and music and the Yukon. Apparently he composed most of the poem in his head before returning to his quarters at the bank. Most of his fellow employees were sound asleep, except for the ledger keeper, a light sleeper. Service tried to tiptoe downstairs to write his poem in the teller's cage, but woke the ledger keeper, who thought Service was a robber. Seeing a dark figure moving near the safe, the ledger keeper reached for his revolver and fired. Fortunately he was a bad shot and only terrified Service. When everyone settled down again for the night, Service continued writing his poem, the lines coming to him faster than he could write them, perhaps stimulated by the adrenaline set off by the shot.

The church declined to let Service read "McGrew" on the grounds that it was a bit coarse for a refined audience, but he kept writing, often composing as he walked, each poem something about the Yukon and its past. Eventually he sent a collection of his poems to a publisher in Scotland who printed them, and he soon became one of the most widely read, recited and parodied poets in North America. For years he was second only to Kipling in popularity among those who like poems that are easy to read or were written to be read aloud.

Many of his poems were based on real incidents, and the most popular one involves the Southerner who could never get warm after moving north. The poem was "The Cremation of Sam McGee." The incident that gave Service the idea involved one of the ugliest steamboats ever to appear on the Yukon River, the *Olive May*. She looked as though her builder had put a pile of big boxes together and launched them.

One year the *Olive May* was wintered in on lower Lake Laberge with a skeleton crew, when an old trapper living nearby became seriously ill. A doctor was brought out from Whitehorse but was unable to save him. After the old man died, they were faced with the usual dilemma of the North when a death occurs during the winter: how to dispose of the body with the ground frozen. The doctor came up with the solution of firing up the boilers in the *Olive May* and cremating the unfortunate in the firebox. Somebody told Service of the incident and he wrote one of his funniest and most popular ballads from the incident. There is hardly a school or amateur drama group in Canada that has not performed it.

But he didn't write the one about the doctor who stayed in the Yukon a number of years and was standing on a barge waving good-bye to his friends at Mayo when he tumbled off into the Stewart River and drowned.

Service is taken very seriously, and an American once started reciting the bastardized version of "McGrew." He was told to shut up, after he had recited the first four lines:

> A bunch of the boys were whooping it up
> In one of the Yukon Halls
> And the man beside the jukebox was steadily
> Scratching his balls . . .

Serious students of Service delight in going over his poems word by word, examining them carefully to discover why he used them (other than the sometimes obvious reason that they rhymed). For example, he did not write that men "toiled" for gold; they "moiled." Dan McGrew did not listen to a ragtime tune; it was a "jagtime" tune.

Whitehorse takes other cultural matters equally seriously. The most popular film ever shown there is *Paint Your Wagon*, which did poorly elsewhere. The theater owner books it in with about the same assurance of good houses that another theater would have in booking *Gone with the Wind*. Nowhere else in North America is the story of raunchy prospectors who sing so popular. Again, it is the Service syndrome: Yukoners like to think of themselves as rugged miners—even Yukoners who work in a bank. When R-rated movies with explicit sex are shown, the theaters are virtually empty, not because people don't care about sex in Whitehorse, they are quick to explain. Rather, it is because they tend to be traditional about such matters, and do not understand voyeurism. As one young man explained, "We take our rye neat and our sex straight."

Copies of Ayn Rand's books are read and reread, borrowed and sometimes stolen in Whitehorse, particularly her giant novel, *Atlas Shrugged.* Its emphasis on the individual, its lack of standard morality and its sermons on the virtue of wealth appeal to a society composed of people fleeing government regulation and rigid social structures in search of a mother lode. Ayn Rand's fantasy of life in a big, secret valley protected by laser beams represents the epitome of freedom to her followers in Whitehorse, a city rapidly becoming as standardized and class-conscious as those its residents fled.

Whitehorse is essentially a government town and observers have noted the inevitable increase in bureaucrats far exceeding the population growth. Whitehorse has more than half of the whole Yukon population of some 20,000, and about half of that population works for the government in some capacity. Since Whitehorse has its own city government separate from the federal territorial government, the friction steadily increases as the federal employees and departments multiply. The territorial council was recently expanded to an even dozen elected members, while the commissioner remains an appointed official by the capital at Ottawa. The usual complaints about federal government—that it does not provide more services as the bureaucrats increase and that it only complicates the citizens' lives with forms—are heard often. The demand that the Yukon Territory become a province, similar to an American state, also is repeated frequently. But Ottawa and many political realists believe the Yukon is neither financially nor emotionally stable enough to support itself. The territorial government receives substantial federal grants for operating expenses that would be shut off should provincial status be granted. The economy, based almost entirely on mining and tourism, does not yield a broad enough tax base to match the federal funds that are pumped into the territory each year. For example, during the 1972–1973 fiscal year, when the total budget was $44.6 million, the federal government gave the Yukon an operating grant of $10.4 million, a sharp increase over the previous year's $6.8 million. So the arguments about territorial versus provincial status continue—and usually heat up when the summer ends and the boredom of winter confinement begins.

By no means have the Yukoners abandoned their British heritage while seeking out new freedoms they feel are no longer available in the provinces. More than any other aspect of the adherence to old values is the Canadians' love of the Queen and the ceremony connected to that office. The Queen's visits to British Commonwealth nations are infrequent, but she is represented in Canada by the Governor General of Canada, the ceremonial head of state who, like the Queen, has no actual power over the people. His office represents to Canadians what the Queen does to England; a symbol above mere politics and day-to-day life with its trivial problems.

When the Governor General visits the provinces and territories it is the social—and perhaps emotional—event of the decade. Prospectors and trappers, who yield to no one, become gentle as infants at the thought of meeting the Queen's representative, and the territories sometimes submit to an orgy of naming landmarks and parks in his honor. When Gilbert John Elliot-Murray-Kynynmond, fourth earl of Minto, the Governor General from 1898 to 1904, visited the Yukon, they named a town, a park, a steamboat and numerous other features and fixtures for him. The footbridge over Miles Canyon was built in 1922 for a Governor General, too; it was the first bridge over the Yukon. Every politician is fair game for Yukoners, and there isn't a single politician on the local or national level who does not take his verbal lumps from voters, but never, never the Queen or her representative. Canadians may complain about Princess Margaret's personality, or about Princess Anne's intelligence, but never the Queen herself or Roland Michener, the Governor General who visited Whitehorse one August. Yet this fascination for royalty is not taken nearly as seriously by the ordinary citizens as by the bureaucrats, nor is it as prevalent in smaller towns as it is in the territorial capital where the populace tends more toward establishing social pecking orders.

Nobody in the Yukon remembers that visit more vividly than Brian Martin, who arrived to work in the information branch of the territorial government one morning and that

71

same day received the assignment to "take care" of the Governor General. It is no wonder he now is back in the concrete canyons of Vancouver. The first assignment, plus mud and dust and suffocating bureaucracy, drove him south before he really intended to leave the Yukon. In spite of the misery it caused him, the Governor General's visit will always be one of the highlights of his life, and he delights in telling of the experience now that the passage of time has worn off the edges of irritation and frustration he suffered.

"The main thing to remember is the pomposity that goes with that kind of office," Martin says, "and what happens to a place like Whitehorse or Dawson City when you suddenly transport that pomposity into it.

"I drove up the Alaska Highway and that very first day they told me the Governor General was coming in August shortly followed by the Prime Minister, followed up by a whole series of cabinet ministers. The North was very in that year. I thought the Prime Minister would be the one to worry about, but that wasn't the case. The Prime Minister gets elected, and he doesn't really give a damn as long as he looks good and has a lot of press along with him.

"The Governor General in this country is the Queen's representative, and I later found out when I went to Ottawa that he lives in a very big house and the Prime Minister lives in a nice house but not nearly as big, and that he does in fact represent royalty. In this country, royalty has its own mystique.

"It struck me as silly for me to take care of it. I'd always thought people who knew what they were doing took care of people like Governor Generals and Prime Ministers. But it is just guys like me who get slugged into the job.

"Later that first afternoon I met Major Deacon, one of three Canadian Armed Forces people in the Yukon Territory, who delivered a book to me on protocol, which I'd never heard of. It was about three inches thick, and it involved who should curtsy, who should shake hands, who should bow and that sort of thing. It was very, very detailed—who could speak to the Governor General first, who spoke second, who spoke third.

72

"Now I was a police reporter from Calgary and that had nothing to do with pomposity. This did.

"Also that same day, Don Sawatsky, whom I love dearly, a tremendous guy, walked into the office to interview my director for CBC and dropped a bunch of books on my desk on the way in; one was by Steinbeck. When he left, he forgot to pick them up. I chased him out into Steele Street and we went across to the Taku Hotel and got very drunk talking about Steinbeck. During the session I suggested he try and get on as a freelance with the department and help me out of this bind—which he did, and away we went.

"I lined up a schedule for the Governor General, which involved most of the Yukon towns—Whitehorse, Mayo, Keno, Dawson City and Old Crow. The whole thing hit the fan when I got a telegram from a fellow named George Thomas, the liaison man between the Department of Northern Development and Indian Affairs and Government House, which in Ottawa is comparable to Buckingham Palace.

"The telegram was just ludicrous. It said I was stupid and that the Governor General couldn't just be in Whitehorse Monday until Wednesday and Keno on Friday or whatever, but every hour of every day had to be accounted for by Telex and had to be approved by His Excellency. That's a term I hadn't run into at that stage.

"The next problem was sleeping arrangements. I assumed the Governor General and his wife, who had been married about forty years, slept together. Very diplomatically, in a long Telex, I was told they didn't and was also informed they had to have separate beds and separate rooms with an adjoining sitting room. There's no such thing in Whitehorse and certainly no such thing outside of Whitehorse. Well!

"And they wanted a pavilion built in Mayo. I didn't know what a pavilion was, but I knew we didn't have one and couldn't build one. I think probably the Arabs have them; you see them in bad movies.

"The territorial government was on an austerity program, and they weren't about to spring the money even for me to drive to Dawson City and visit the town first. I'd never bloody well been there, so I had to get a map of downtown Dawson City from the tourist department and plot out a parade route for them.

"His Excellency was arriving in a Boeing 707 and bringing thirty-six people with him, plus the press corps. I went to bed one night and collapsed in the middle of this mess and I woke up from a sound sleep—honest to God, I had a vision that there was no way a 707 was going to land in Whitehorse. I'd just finished reading a book called *Airlines, Airports, and You* about weight factors and how much room they need to take off, and I knew nobody in Ottawa had thought of this. I got on the phone and started tracking down the pilot in Ottawa and finally found him in the officer's mess, and he allowed as how he had no idea whether they could land a 707 in Whitehorse but he'd certainly check on it. He called back with the news that, first of all, yes, he could land; it was doubtful he could take off, though. But they could take off with half fuel so they could go on to Edmonton or Vancouver from Whitehorse. Then, offhandedly, he asked if we had a starting engine for a 707.

"I'm a reporter—how in Christ could I know that 707's required starting engines? In a car you put the key in, and I later found that in the smaller 737's you can do the trick with a key or whatever else you have to use. But the 707 has to have a big truck that backs up to it to turn the first jet that turns the second jet.

"So I phoned the airport manager, who said he didn't have a starting engine, and that he didn't really give a damn. The Governor General is coming up and that's *his* problem. He was a typical Yukoner.

"Ottawa finally said they could get around it by not turning off all the engines. They would turn off only the engines on the side he'd be getting off, fly the bloody thing to Vancouver where they could land the bloody thing and shut off the engines, then come back to Whitehorse and pick him up. All we had to do was supply the steps.

"Bingo again!

"Boeing 737's, which fly all over the North, are self-contained and have their own steps. But 707's don't. Back to the

74

airport manager. He still doesn't care. So I'm worried about this and call the fire department, because I've seen one of those cherrypicker things that go up and down. There's no bloody way I'm going to stand on the Whitehorse airport tarmac and yell, 'Jump, Your Excellency. I'll catch you.' No way. He represents twelve hundred years of royalty all the way back to the Magna Carta. My parents are British and they wouldn't allow me to do that.

"So I thought that, if worse came to worse, I could pluck His and Her Excellency off the plane with the cherrypicker, then rig an emergency chute for the others. Surely to Christ their underlings could do that. I told the guys at the fire hall and they laughed but said they'd be glad to do that for us. No sweat. Sure: 'Buy us a beer on Saturday night.' "

Brian called the vocational school and arranged for them to build steps, but he had to find the measurements somewhere —then George Thomas, the liaison man, entered the picture again.

"His concern wasn't that a 707 could or could not land in Whitehorse. He was worried because he said that under no circumstances would the Governor General and his Lady walk down the same steps as the staff. The 707 comes with two doors and His and Her Excellency come out the front and the staff out the back door.

"And Thomas was worried about cars. When you think about it, there are very few cars in Whitehorse because thirty percent of the guys I know drive pickups, as I did at the time, and twenty percent are civil servants who never bothered buying cars. The rest have cars, but they're beat up and have broken windows and beer bottles in the back seat. And the Governor General, of course, required a limousine for himself and a limousine for his wife—they don't ride in the same car. He rides in the right rear seat and his wife rides in the right rear seat of the next car, and the rest follow in a descending order.

"The cars would be, preferably, Cadillacs, and the staff in smaller cars and the press could use a school bus. So I got busy renting ordinary green Chevrolets for the staff. But I really went bananas for the Governor General and decided, if they were going to be that snotty, I'd come up with a limousine.

"There's only two or three guys in the whole Yukon who have Cadillacs, outside of Al Kulan, who at the time had his Rolls-Royce. I didn't know him and wasn't about to ask him for it. However, there was a local Chevrolet dealer who had one Cadillac that had been in the showroom for some time. It was an ordinary, everyday dark blue Cadillac sedan and I asked him to lend it to us. He was really upset, because one of the stipulations was that the Alaska Highway through Whitehorse had to be oiled—it was a gravel road then. His Excellency couldn't ride in the dust. Of course there was no way the dealer was going to let his Cadillac be driven over fresh oil. But we got that all sorted out and thought the problem of cars was solved, until George Thomas got back into the act. 'You realize, of course, you have to drill a hole for the Governor General's pennant in the right front wing.' I didn't even know what the right front wing was, but when I found out I knew I was supposed to go back and talk the dealer into letting us drill a bloody hole in the front fender. No way. This I explained to Ottawa at the top of my lungs, and George hung up on me. I called the Governor General's secretary, a great guy who had run into this sort of bureaucracy before, and he told me to forget it; he'd take care of everything. And he did, as we shall see.

"Then we had to have a security meeting with the Royal Canadian Mounted Police in Whitehorse. Sawatsky and I walked across the street together because I wouldn't go alone on that one. They canceled the meeting because Don was there. Apparently Don had some kind of misunderstanding with one of the Mounties while he was a reporter for CBC, and they didn't want anything to do with him. We finally got that straightened out and they accepted him, then some RCMP guy whipped open a briefcase with some papers and started on me.

"I'd worked for a very small newspaper, the *Alaska Highway News* in Fort St. John, and the paper had run some very conservative editorials from a propaganda agency something like the John Birch Society. It was really hate literature, bad stuff. We had reprinted them verbatim but I had also written an editorial that week saying the publisher had taken control of the editorial page although I was editor, and that I, as editor, had nothing to do with that.

"I was really amazed that the RCMP had clipped all those things. Who really cares? It really makes me wonder what the RCMP is doing in Ottawa. Apparently one thing they're doing is clipping every rural weekly paper in Canada."

Then Brian began working on the state reception, which would be the largest function ever held in Whitehorse. He had to find some way to sit eight hundred people down in one place and feed them and make it look good. The government still wouldn't tell him what kind of budget he had, except that he wasn't to spend much.

"The Commissioner said, and this is a direct quote: 'Brian, we've got to make it glitter.' How do you make it glitter in Whitehorse? And where in Whitehorse can you sit eight hundred people down? The only place we could do that was in the Whitehorse Recreation Center, an old building left by the military in World War II out by the airport. It didn't glitter. It was ugly. It had the basketball things painted on the floor and it was all scratched and ugly. I gave Sawatsky the assignment to make it glitter.

"He decided to panel it with mahogany, and I authorized it because I thought, Wow! When we're through we're going to have a rec center that looks like a lawyer's office. That was fine until the manager informed us that the day after this big ball, they had some kind of major sports event and the paneling was going to have to go. That's sort of fairy, you know. They'd look like fags in Whitehorse. What kind of club is this?

"A local church group catered the dinner. There was one oven at the rec center and Brian Martin was all over town borrowing ovens and turkeys and had half the people lined up to bake turkey that day.

"I thought it would be a neat idea if we decorated all the tables with flowers. I went one step farther. The only flower that is in bloom in the summer is the Yukon official flower, the fireweed, so I hopped in my pickup and began looking for a big fireweed patch. I found one very near the rec center on the Alaska Highway and had a friend post guard over it and signed up a couple of girls from the office to bring them in the back door as the guests were arriving in the front, because fireweed doesn't last long.

"Everyone was very nervous and stirred up to the point that the Commissioner's wife was worried about how to curtsy. I'd sent a Telex to Ottawa asking about this and got one back saying this was dropped in 1962 or something and that you don't have to curtsy anymore. That was brought on by embarrassment with local people falling on their ass. Most people don't know how to curtsy and if you don't know how, don't do it. I know. Sawatsky and I tried it in the office in case we had to teach people. A quick bow from the waist. Not from the middle or from the knees, but from the waist.

"We got everything ready, and it was my first experience with Ottawa's stupidity on time zones. Everything in the world revolves around Ottawa time. They completely blew it and were hours off on the time they should arrive in Whitehorse.

"It's very obvious when a 707 arrives in Whitehorse— like a prehistoric bird it darkens the sky over the town. I was in the government office and saw this huge thing coming up over Gray Mountain and I went right off my chair, down the steps into my car, and got to the airport when they were just landing and taxiing back from the end of the field.

"I called Marie Slater, the Commissioner's secretary, and told her they arrived two hours early and get the Commissioner out here. The Commissioner's wife was in a beauty parlor getting her hair set and they yanked her from under the dryer. And we had to have a band to pipe him in, and the only band in Whitehorse was the Midnight Sun Pipe Band. The whole thing took only about twelve minutes. Everyone saw this plane come in and dashed out.

"We got everybody all lined up. The pipe band knew only one song, but nobody had thought of what happens to a pipe band when they can turn off only two engines on a 707. You can't hear it, and at the same time CP Air has fired up its 737 engines for the afternoon flight.

"When the Governor General arrives, you have to play 'God Save the Queen.' It is a necessity. When he comes to the door of the plane they strike up the band, he proceeds halfway down the steps, where he stands at attention until they complete it; then His Excellency, followed by Her Excellency, followed by . . . by . . . by . . . down the descending order—all proceed to the tarmac where they're to be introduced.

"They're all coming down and everything was cool. The Governor General stood at the front door of the plane waving just like the Queen does, gently like he's holding a fan, but couldn't go any farther because he couldn't hear his cue, the music.

"This whole thing is theater, and good theater when it's done well, but we weren't doing it well. This show wasn't going to be a hit if somebody didn't turn off that jet engine so he could hear the music. Just then CP Air released their passengers from the terminal for their flight, and when they saw what was going on, they all diverted with their Instamatics beneath the jets. This was driving the RCMP bananas because—who knows? —that geologist might have a Molotov cocktail in his briefcase. RCMP is following orders, too, and they have to do it right.

"The Governor General can't shut his motors off or he'll never get out of town, and it's written all over his face that all he wants out of life at this moment is to hear 'God Save the Queen' so he can get the hell out of here and into his car. And he couldn't. The band was looking at me for direction and after they played the only tune they knew, 'William Nae Go Home,' they started 'God Save the Queen.' Nowadays in Canada they don't play the whole thing; only the first eight bars, but they were going to play the whole thing.

"I motioned to the band to stop and waved to the Governor General to come down because he still couldn't hear. He was a great guy.

"While all this is going on I'm still terrified about those pennants, which I don't have. So the secretary pulls one out of his fancy suit, licks the suction cup, and sticks it on the right front wing. It lasted the whole trip and finally fell off another car in Dawson. Some native kid probably still has it as a souvenir.

"So we got the Governor General on the right-hand side of the rear seat and an RCMP guy on the right-hand side of the front seat and the Commissioner on the left-hand side of the rear seat, Her Excellency on the right-hand side of the rear seat of the second car and Mrs. Smith on the left-hand side of the rear seat of the second car.

"Then came the unmarked police car, and that was silly in the Yukon; everyone in town knew he was an undercover cop because they curl with him all winter and play basketball with him all summer. Today you can't recognize him. You can't say, 'Hi, George,' because he's undercover that day.

"We had an RCMP guy drive the Cadillac and it has been checked for bombs. In Whitehorse they can't make a carburetor work, let alone a bomb."

With the Governor General finally in town, the crises seemed to increase. The manager of the Travelodge, where His Excellency stayed, was upset because he hadn't been told a cook traveled with the entourage and expected to cook His Excellency's meals (he did not), and the civil servants hadn't been told there were no three-room suites available.

And there was a crisis over the Governor General's survival kit—it wouldn't go through the Travelodge doors. It was a large wooden box about 10 feet long and 4 or 5 feet high, which Brian thought was a little silly because "if the 707 hits a mountain you won't be needing it."

While all the disputes were occurring on the ground, a backup plane circled overhead constantly. Brian assumed it had to come down for refueling sometime, but he said every time he looked up, it was there, like an airborne Flying Dutchman.

When it came time for the banquet, glitter and all, they had to have a photograph of Her Majesty and the Duke of Edinburgh—"Otherwise Buckingham Palace would crumble and all fall down. Except for some small photos in little old ladies' bedrooms over in Riverdale, the only photos in Whitehorse were hanging in the Territorial Council Chambers.

"So we got a key and took the photos and the flags—the Union Jack, the Canadian flag and the Territorial flag. They have to be crossed the right way. Sawatsky and I drew a map— we weren't totally dumb—hauled them up to the rec center and arranged them in their proper sequence. The Queen's picture had to be exactly one quarter inch above the Duke's picture.

For some reason I knew that. It's just one of those trivial stupid things you know.

"We had it all set up and everything was beautiful—but we made a tragic mistake. We had forgotten to note that the Governor General visited the territorial council chambers before he went to the banquet. Halfway through town this hits me. We've just destroyed that room and we can't take him in there. The Queen is gone because she's been hijacked to the rec center. So I dispatched Sawatsky right in the middle of the parade in a government car to the rec center—'I don't care if you gotta break the door down, get in there and get all those pictures and flags to the council chambers exactly the way they were.'

"So we get to the Federal Building and we've got the elevator operator on duty on the weekend. There are three elevators in the Yukon; one in the hospital, one in the Lynn Building and one in the Federal Building—and that one is sort of a problem because there's only one elevator operator in the Yukon, and if she's sick you don't ride.

"We're going up in that elevator and I'm thinking; 'Oh, please, Don, have those flags up there.' We opened the door and everything was there, except the Queen was hanging at about a forty-five-degree angle and she looked like she's about four sheets to the wind.

"I sidled up behind the speaker's chair in the front of the chambers, reached up and corrected her. But unfortunately I overcorrected and she was about forty-five degrees the other way. Sawatsky's out in the hallway cackling to himself. I tell him to get those goddamned things back to the rec center, and as they go out the door, there's Don taking flags down. He dashes down the back steps and away he goes.

"The banquet went off like a gem, except for one small thing. The Commissioner's secretary, through no fault of her own, bought a dress that was almost identical to the Governor General's wife's. So there was a bit of a ripple there. We also had to present the Governor General with a buckskin coat which was stinking to high heaven. They're handmade in Indian houses, and they're all smoked and urinated on and it smelled up the back seat of my car.

"So we've got fireweed and Sawatsky coming in the back door with the picture of the Queen. Again. She's been all over Whitehorse that day. We sat down and someone had my truck running all over Whitehorse picking up turkey.

"I had a very classic type of civil service director who was pompous as hell and didn't know what was going on. It was a status thing to travel with the Governor General, and everyone wanted to go. He had invited a lot of friends and we had twenty-three seats on the plane, and I'd told him at least a dozen times: twenty-three, not twenty-four. Nobody extra. Two-three. That night we had exactly twenty-three—but he invited his girl friend at the banquet. I walked straight across the hall to a guy who ran a charter service and chartered a plane for Sawatsky and myself, grabbed a local radio guy to go with us, and we had our own party.

"The next morning about seven thirty, we're heading for Dawson. The Commissioner and Governor General are traveling in the Caribou and the staff and press were in a DC3. There also was the armed forces surveillance plane, and Don Sawatsky and Brian Martin were in their private twin-engine aircraft directing this whole thing. I felt like Howard Hughes.

"We had a hell of a time with the cars in Dawson City. They were all old cars, so I went up and found one of the rental agencies that was run by a mechanic. I found him in a pit—he didn't have a hoist—and I was yelling down to him trying to arrange for a rental and he was trying to explain to me that he didn't take reservations, that it was on a first-come basis because he'd once lost twenty dollars when someone didn't show. I tried to explain that the Governor General was good for his money. He wouldn't do it, so I had to bring them in from Whitehorse, rentals and volunteers.

"I never did see what happened in Mayo, but Don and I had this funny pilot. He was very pleasant but apparently he wasn't very experienced. I was in the back and Don in the front, and when he came into Dawson the plane flipped over and we went over the Klondike River upside down and Don was yelling at the pilot at the top of his lungs because Don knew what he had done: he'd come in with the wind. The bloody pilot said, 'Shit! I could have sworn that wind sock was going the other way.'

"Nobody was there. There's not even an airport there, just that little wooden shack. The Northward Aviation agent said, 'Oh, they're coming out from Dawson. Don't worry.' I worried. The first to arrive was the mayor, a great guy, who was pretty upset about all this and flustered. He had a 1968 Chrysler hardtop Imperial with one window broken and plywood in it instead of glass. I explained what he was doing and that he had to ride back with the Governor General—and what was he doing with his car twelve miles out? So he gives me the keys to his Chrysler. That's cool. I'll drive his car back. He's excited and can't remember if he's speaking French or English, which is fine because the Governor General is bilingual. His wife is there: I love her, but she's at least three hundred pounds, and she's not quite up to this. She has an eight-millimeter movie camera and is shoving it in the face of everybody who moves. The mayor has a can of beer in his back pocket and she has the camera. I'm going to have to offend somebody. The camera they'll forgive but not the beer, so I hooked it out of his back pocket and threw it to Sawatsky, who probably drank it.

"A DC3 came over the horizon, and I knew it wasn't the Governor General. It landed, and it's making a lot of noise and dust on the gravel strip and I'm trying to tell them to relax, it's not the right guy. But the mayor jumps up and starts shaking hands with the first guy who comes off the DC3. I think he was from UPI or something, he was certainly a member of the press, and he thought it was quite funny. I didn't.

"Then the bloody Caribou arrived. The Caribou has a very short takeoff and landing, but it had trouble landing in Dawson City because they dropped it short of the airstrip by about fifteen feet. It went into the bush right at the end and the leaves flew and I just about wet myself.

"Don is with me, to catch me when I fainted, and I said, 'Shit, they've killed him.' Then the plane came bounding through this stuff and landed on the airstrip and there's corruption flying in all directions. There was hell to pay later and another air crew came in to replace them. Nobody was in any great danger of being hurt. On an ordinary military flight those things can go down in the willow bush and come up smiling. But you do not dump the Governor General and his lady in the willow bush.

"Another thing that happened on that flight: when they're flying or anywhere with limited facilities, nobody can use the can until the Governor General's wife has used the can; until the royal bottom has sat upon the seat, it cannot be sullied. Apparently all the way from Whitehorse to Dawson City she didn't have to go. And people were dying. 'For god's sake, woman, just go in and powder your face so the rest of us can.' I imagine there were a few problems when that thing hit the bush because there were a few guys who didn't need that right then.

"They taxied up and everyone bounded down and the mayor's wife shoved the camera in everyone's face. This was going great, because suddenly everything was so silly and out of kilter that it was much nicer than in Whitehorse where we were trying so hard to be polite and proper. In Dawson City we hadn't even tried to get a Cadillac. The secretary still had the flag and—bang!—he planted it on the fender of the Chevy I had. We got everything lined up and ready for the parade into Dawson City, and I had to get the mayor's car back. I got into this Christly thing, which is a monument. It has a cockpit with all those chrome buttons you push. In days gone by you pushed one and the windows went up and down but now it has a sheet of plywood which doesn't go up and down. But you couldn't start the thing because the key goes in at a funny angle and the starter is under the gas pedal like the old Buick, and you also had to get the buttons in the right place, the right ones pushed in and the right ones pulled out. So I'm the only guy who knows where they're going. Even the Commissioner doesn't know because Sawatsky and I are carrying the itinerary around in our back pockets. They're all going down the road without me, and the RCMP are leading and not knowing where they're going and I'm still pushing these crazy buttons. All of a sudden there's this awful roar and all five hundred horses leaped into control. I caught up with them and started passing them, passing police cars trying to work my way to the front. Suddenly

84

there's somebody with an American license plate in a VW van with all sorts of peace things and doves on it and knapsacks and crap on the roof. He thinks this is cool. Man, oh wow. He's right on my tail the whole way and we're sucking in the Governor General of Canada and this kid in a VW is right on my rear bumper. He won't go away.

"The RCMP sees us. Here's this old beat-up hotrod and an American VW bus, so he's going to get us. He pulls out of line and I'm turning around waving him back into line. 'Stay there. For five minutes I'm your boss!' He got the message, which is a credit to the RCMP.

"I got in front on the Ogilvie Bridge and the VW did the same thing and we arrived at the Robert Service Motel, me leading the parade and some poor American kid wanting to see the North. I asked him to screw off, and he went, just like that. My voice was a little hysterical: 'You get out of here!'

"The manager of the motel had actually gone so far as to put in wall-to-wall carpeting and bought new beds and bed sets, and everything was beautiful. There was no place to feed everyone inside, so we had picnic tables all set up in the parking lot. We served the Governor General and his wife in their cabin and everybody else ate outside on picnic tables.

"Mrs. Michener came out to see me, of all people, and all those Ottawa people were standing up. I was sitting there with my face in my potato salad, so zonked by everything that it never crossed my mind that everyone was standing up. She walked straight up to me and said sweetly, 'Don't rise.' She was a really nice woman.

"We had to do a Dawson tour. It was Discovery Day weekend and I had laid on an hour for the Discovery Day parade. We would all assemble on the decks of the *Keno*— once a steamboat and now a museum—where they would 're-view' the parade. Although they went around the block twice in honor of the Governor General, the parade took about twelve minutes, which left most of an hour to kill.

"Everybody was getting drunk. There was this woman with enormous breasts who worked in one of those touristy things and she was on a float that was just a Mack truck with a flatbed, one of those Cassiar asbestos mine trucks. I don't know what else she had on. All I remember is that they were decent when viewed from ground level. But viewed from the top of the *Keno* looking straight down, they were not decent because they were large and there was no covering over all the material that was her. So as she went by she looked straight up at the Governor General, took one of those breasts and pushed it up from the bottom. It popped out and she yelled, 'How do you like that, Guv?' I just about fainted. He didn't flinch.

"I could see my driver disappear over to a hot dog stand and the parade had ended and my car was in the next block behind. I got into an RCMP car: 'Here we go, turn right at the next corner.' The Mountie was very new to Dawson and we got lost. It was a Rambler and I hadn't been in the back seat of a police cruiser since I was fifteen when I got the hell scared out of me and sent home and licked by my father. I'd forgotten they saw off the handles in the back seat, and he'd gotten himself lost. The whole parade went down one of those old muddy roads. The Mountie is upset and nervous. I decided I wasn't going to stick with him anymore and I reached for the bloody door handle and it was sawed off. He slammed on the brakes and I slid over the front seat on my belly and onto his radio equipment sitting on the seat, then went out the passenger side and ran down the street after the parade. Soon I gave up and walked. Pretty soon they came back. It was Katzenjammer Kids. It was all mixed up with the Governor General's car way down the list when he should have been in front.

"The first car is Bruce Harvey, the National Historic Sites guy. I knew him and I was embarrassed. I can't let the one guy in the parade I know see me, the leader of the parade, running up the street the other way. So I opened the door of a house, stepped into the living room and closed the door. Luckily I was in a welfare place guys use as a crash pad. There were all those guys in their sleeping bags looking up at me. I said, 'Excuse me.' The parade went by and I stepped back outside and closed the door again.

"I got myself another government car and joined the parade. The first thing I caught up with was Mrs. Michener's car with the hood up. This car is not going to start, so I said, 'Your Excellency, would you please get into my car?' She did, but Her Excellency decided halfway to the park she was not well. You know: 'We are not well.' But what I think she wanted to say was that 'We have had bloody well enough.' I returned her to Robert Service where a lady-in-waiting was waiting. She disappeared into her motel, which was clean and carpeted and cool and dark and away from all these madmen in Dawson who were running in all directions.

"I beat it back to Minto Park where everything was as boring as you would expect it to be. Everyone gave speeches that went on forever and ever and bloody ever. There was almost no audience because they'd all gathered there and within five minutes they'd all gone away to drink beer again.

"The following day was a day of rest, and the Governor General and his wife were to go to a wilderness camp on the Pelly River. They were to fly there from Dawson until I get a Telex from Ottawa saying that the Governor General does not fly in a single-engine aircraft. It had to be a twin-engine plane, and there was no way you could land a twin-engine aircraft there. Someone found a Grumman Goose over in Yellowknife and we were going to use it—until Alan Innes-Taylor looked over my shoulder in the office and pointed out that if they landed that thing at the camp they'd all be killed. There's seven feet of water there and the plane takes twelve.

"So we arranged for them to fly from Dawson to the Minto airstrip, where they would be picked up in a boat. I'd also had a Telex from Ottawa saying it had to be an enclosed launch. The boat wasn't enclosed, so they compromised and said the Governor General had to wear rubber clothing. I borrowed that from the Fisheries Department. So I dressed them up in rubber clothing and away they went. They were no longer my problem because they would allow nobody to go with them. They kept the secretary and an RCMP and that was it.

"Sawatsky and I felt sorry for the other staff and decided to take them on a river trip with Captain Dick Stevenson. The mayor contributed fifteen cases of beer to the cause (over his wife's dead body, I might add), and we headed down the Yukon River. That was fun. We went to Moosehide and drank all the beer, which was a mistake. We were quite high when we got back on the boat, and Dick took us to his fish wheel [a water-wheel gadget that traps fish in the flat spokes and drops them in a holding pen]. There were quite a few RCMP aboard, including Inspector Woods from Vancouver, who was sent up to mastermind this whole thing. One of them made a bad mistake. He wanted a close look at a fish wheel and stepped on it. When you step on a fish wheel it goes under the water. That sobered everybody up in a hurry, because the last we saw of this particular constable was him going under the Yukon. That's a very dirty, swift, cold river. He was gone. That was it. He wasn't there anymore. That wheel just turned the other way and what had been under the river was straight up. And that constable was underneath the water.

"I was scared. I'd arranged for the boat and the beer. I've had a RCMP constable drown and CBC is on board and CPTV is there, and a few smaller ones. Thank God for Inspector Wood. The RCMP really do train their men well. He stood up and issued orders for everyone to shut up and sit still. Everyone froze. He reached under the water, found this guy, grabbed hold of his clothes and yanked him over the edge. The whole thing took probably ten seconds.

"God love Dick Stevenson, but he was unaffected by it and he was willing to continue the tour: '. . . And on your right you see the wrecked boats that were brought up in 1931. . . .'

" 'Dick, the party's over,' I yelled. 'Back to Dawson right now.'

"Government people on government money drunk in the Yukon river with a drowned RCMP constable? The Commissioner would have killed me. We've gone to all this trouble and spent all this money, and things have gone so well in spite of everything that's happened—and we drown a goddamn Mountie when the Governor General isn't even in town. It was a real Queen Victoria 'we are not amused' situation.

"I didn't get to go on the Old Crow visit. There were no cars there because there were no roads. But we did get a truck in. The territorial government had taken one part way in the winter before. I don't know how they got it there, either over a muskeg road or winched in. It was just a GMC pickup and used now by the Native Brotherhood to haul wood. The bureaucrats had insisted we supply a chauffeur in Old Crow. That's really silly. Nobody had a driver's license in Old Crow. There was no possible reason they would have one. We got a kid who learned to drive in Whitehorse and paid him ten dollars as chauffeur to drive that pickup to the airstrip at Old Crow, just a few feet from the village.

"The Indians at Old Crow had washed that truck until the sun just glinted off it.

"When they got there, the Governor General's wife elected to walk. This was a big disappointment to the kid because he didn't get to drive. He did get a check for ten dollars.

"The Governor General enjoyed himself enormously when I wasn't there—or people like me weren't there—to screw things up. When things weren't going right he took things in hand himself. Apparently he was quite unhappy that he hadn't been allowed more time in Old Crow.

"From Old Crow they went to Inuvik. They still had those bloody rubber suits, and the fisheries people were after me to get them back. I put through a call to Inuvik at the one pay phone in Dawson—it's on a pole like 'Green Acres' on television, and you climb up to it. I got through and the line went dead. The operator said the line had been out all day until I explained to her that I'd just been talking to them and she said she could route it through Hay River. So hello, Whitehorse, hello Edmonton, hello Hay River, hello Inuvik. *I want my pants!*

"You know, he sent them collect. The government wouldn't accept the voucher. The Governor General still owes me eight dollars. Even. Not eight dollars and twelve cents, but eight dollars."

Brian never felt totally at ease in the Yukon and always believed the Governor General's trip put a jinx on his career. As much as he enjoyed Dawson City, he had a series of misfortunes there that gave credence to the jinx theory. He once went to Dawson City on a press trip and discovered on arrival in the hotel he had brought an empty suitcase, "and I walked across the street to the dry goods store and told them to give me a toothbrush, a tube of Crest, two pairs of shorts, and razor —with which I considered ending it all." He moved to Vancouver to edit a magazine and the cloud of misfortune mysteriously lifted.

When we left Whitehorse in a boat headed north, we planned to camp that night on Lake Laberge—one of the highlights of the trip, we believed. We had read Service's "The Cremation of Sam McGee," which made us anxious to camp "on the marge of Lake Laberge." We also had read the poignant account of how it was named: of how Mike Laberge, working on a survey crew of the old Collins Telegraph project, spoke often and longingly of a big beautiful lake upstream that he never got to see.

We cast off into the water running high and swift amid beer cans, plastic wrappers and other garbage pitched into the river or swept off the banks, turned a slight bend and saw a wall of garbage near the river. It was the Whitehorse city dump, with garbage slowly, steadily draining into the river. Somewhere nearby the untreated sewage from the capital also enters the river via a large pipe. It was a little sickening, and we did not dare touch our faces with our hands until we pulled into the mouth of the Takhini River for lunch.

At one time the fishing was as good in Lake Laberge as any other lake along the 60th Parallel, but the fish died as Whitehorse grew and the volume of raw sewage pumped into the river increased. As we neared the shore of Richthofen Island, where we planned to camp, we saw long shreds of slime waving from the underwater rocks like eel grass.

The shores of Laberge have become littered over the past several decades with floatable garbage—old tires, plastic containers, bottles, cans, scraps of lumber—until it would take years to return it to its natural state. The lake is beautiful as advertised until one looks directly beneath one's feet or closely at the lake's bottom. Then it becomes little more than a sewage lagoon. For those attracted to the Yukon by that magical Service line, "the marge of Lake Laberge," polluting the lake with no attempts to clean it seems an obscenity.

As is typical with governments all over the world, millions of dollars are spent on office buildings, four-color brochures, bureaucratic empire building and other government

90

trappings rather than tending to such basic good-manner projects as burying or cleansing human and industrial excrement. Fortunately, the river cleanses itself in Lake Laberge, but for 50 miles the boaters are traveling on little more than diluted sewage.

Just as traces of the gold rush are gone from the river, so too are most signs of the steamboats that worked the river afterward. We expected more visible history than the Yukon River was prepared to give.

Little has been written about the steamboat era in the Yukon by historians, for whom the gold rush is infinitely more appealing and dramatic. But for fifty-odd years the steamboats were as much a way of life as airplanes and automobiles are today. Except for the stubs of piling along the river below Whitehorse, and the restored *Klondike* paddlewheeler, which was built as an ore carrier, there is no hint of the steamboat years where the major depot for the entire Yukon River system stood. They were fascinating pieces of marine architecture, and steamboat buffs speak fondly of those years and dismiss the gold-rush flotilla as a one-shot deal that was more pathetic and insane than romantic.

Steamboats of one kind or another had been on the river more than a decade before the gold rush. The first was brought up by Ed Schiefflin, the discoverer of the Tombstone mine who became uneasy as a wealthy businessman rather than as a prospector. His little paddlewheeler had the innocently accurate name of *New Racket;* indeed, nothing quite like a steamboat had been on the river before to frighten the game and amaze the population. It didn't take long for the canny rivermen to find that the popular sidewheelers of the Mississippi River would never do on the Yukon. The sidewheelers did not respond to steering fast enough, they were easy to entangle in the brush and trees along the shore, and they required a wharf for docking—a luxury most towns never got around to giving themselves.

Paddlewheelers, on the other hand, were responsive to steering, and they could perform with the paddles dropping only 6 inches beneath the hull and nose into any bank the skipper chose. While there were steamboats of every size and

91

description on the river over the years, a more or less typical design came into being: about 125 feet long with a thirty-foot beam, a flat bottom with no external keel, and a variety of interior trusses of timbers and chains and cables to keep the vessels from becoming swaybacked. Perhaps the most important development was a three- or four-story boat that would draw no more than 4 feet of water fully loaded.

The skippers and crew were remarkably resourceful and the boats were adapted and modified for the river as occasion demanded. They had winches on the bow, called a grasshopper, to pull themselves off or even across sandbars. The paddles were sturdy enough to keep slapping away when the winch was pulling, throwing gravel and sand wildly behind.

The crews ranged from a dozen to twenty men, and they almost always had one stationed on the top deck to douse fires caused by sparks and flaming chunks of wood that spewed from the stack.

During the winter months some were pulled out of the river onto ways in Whitehorse, and others were stored in sloughs away from the river to avoid damage or sinking during breakup. When the ice starts moving on the river, it sometimes piles up in monstrous, dangerous stacks of iceberglike chunks that could tear an entire side out of a boat when it suddenly began moving again. While the boats were wintering over in the sloughs, a small crew, sometimes only one man, stayed aboard all winter as watchman and protector, and repairs often were made by the black gangs. As spring approached, the crews came aboard and cut trenches in the ice all around the hull so the boat would be floating free when the ice began breaking and moving.

The boats were usually held in place by spars propped against the hull, which also kept them off the bottom. Should they freeze to the mud, they could easily sink at breakup, because the ice frequently creates a dam with a vast lake behind it. Another trick for breakup safety was partially flooding the hull then shooting steam into the water to heat it and melt the ice against the hull. The boats had an insatiable appetite for wood—so much so that the White Pass & Yukon Route switched to oil long before the boats went out of service. The good spruce timber had been chopped down along the river, while the paddlewheelers consumed an estimated 300,000 cords of 4-foot-length wood.

We saw the first traces of steamboats at the head of Lake Laberge, the old piling slowly rotting away or being covered over with silt. A little farther down the lake we saw a wooden pyramid about 10 feet tall on the south end of Richthofen Island, the red paint still showing on the horizontal boards. We stopped to investigate, but found no place for a lighted beacon to be hung. Then someone in the party remembered that when the steamboats ran—from June to early September—there was virtually no darkness and no need for a lighted beacon.

The skippers soon became masters at "reading" the water and never made the mistake of assuming a channel that existed the previous season would still be there. The river course changes from season to season, sometimes slightly from week to week, and no Corps of Engineers dredge ever chewed up the river bed. A retired skipper drew up a set of maps as a general guide, which the government copies and gives to boaters by the hundreds; but the channel markings are totally useless.

We carried a set of the maps with us and found them useful for geographical information and for configurations along Lake Laberge and the river itself. But, like the steamboats for which they were drawn, they were little more than museum exhibits.

Fort Selkirk

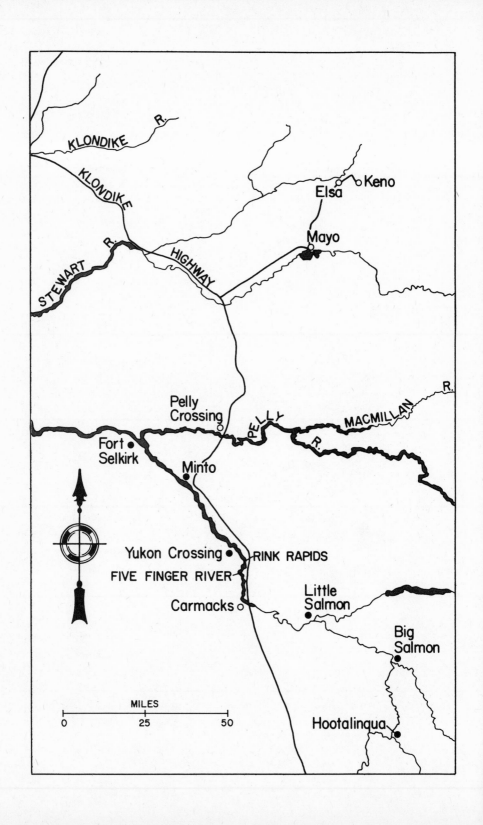

The river pours out of Lake Laberge clear, pure and swift, twisting and turning like a waltz into the canyons of the only true wilderness stretch between Whitehorse and Dawson City. The timber here was never grazed over by the steamboat woodcutters and the river is so swift and the canyon wall so steep that people never bothered settling along it.

Although the river is officially the Yukon all the way from Marsh Lake, sentimentalists still call the Laberge-to-Hootalinqua stretch the Old Thirtymile River. The first maps showed the Yukon beginning far downstream where the Pelly enters at Fort Selkirk, and the river above as far as one cared to travel was the Lewes. Later the Yukon designation was moved upstream to Hootalinqua, where the eastern branch was named the Teslin and the western the Thirtymile to Lake Laberge. The Lewes ran from Marsh Lake to the south end of Laberge. The Thirtymile was named for an obvious reason: its approximate length. It was something of a throwback in the river nomenclature system, for the other rivers were named for their distance from Fort Reliance, the first trading post established by traders in the Yukon. The post was about 6 miles downstream from where Dawson City grew, and being more interested in the distances they had to pole and track boats than in imaginative or honorary names, the early prospectors named rivers by their distance from Fort Reliance—hence the Fortymile and the Sixtymile. These names have survived the ravages of late arrivals, who often seem intent on naming everything in sight for friends, commanding officers, politicians, wives, or each other. There has never been much of a rush to fill the maps with names in the Yukon Territory; so vacant were the maps that the government in the early 1970s felt compelled to begin naming peaks for people who were prominent during the territory's pioneer years and sought public participation in selecting the names.

Fires have swept the Old Thirtymile, as they have virtually every acre of the Yukon Territory south of timberline, but the fast, crooked stream runs through deep canyons beneath virgin timber and past small glades that have not been altered. The river almost curves back on itself in places, and the bank alternates between sheer cliffs of granite walls and clay and limestone wind-carved into fantastic shapes that resemble minarets on a castle built by an Austrian madman. An occasional bald eagle soars above, and swallows by the thousand nest along the cliffs and flutter frantically when disturbed. Moose and bear are often startled by boats, and normal speaking tones rebound from the canyon walls.

We stopped to pick flowers and wild chives, the latter to enliven a salad that night, and returned to the boats looking like a group of Benjy Compsons or Ferdinand the Bulls with the delicate blue and white flowers clutched in dirty, scratched fists.

Most of the Yukon River is silent, but here it makes all the noises one expects of a river. Its narrow walls with pure water rushing over boulders and cobbles, and the pike pursued by its shadow on the bottom, give it a personality, an intimacy the river lacks as it swells with each feeder stream. But the Old Thirtymile is the juvenile portion of the Yukon, and rivers, like all living things, must mature and thicken and accept the burden and routine of middle age.

This juvenile exuberance ends abruptly when the flat, silt-laden Teslin enters. The bottom disappears. The cliffs yield to rolling hills and broad, flat benches behind the banks with almost impenetrable groves of willow, balsam, poplar and wild roses.

One soon learns to avoid the flat river banks because voracious mosquitoes inhabit them in dark, whining clouds, intent on finding blood to insure that their brief lives will be long enough to lay eggs in the still marsh pools and moose hoofprints filled with water. The Scourge of the North had been no particular problem to us, however, and we were not bothered by them while moving on the river. When we stopped for overnight camps we always chose an exposed spot where the wind could hit us because mosquitoes are powerless against the slightest breeze. But we gave ourselves frequent splashes of repellent to coat our skins with a sticky film which attracted dirt while repelling insects.

We received our ration of misery when we stopped for lunch at Yukon Crossing. Although there was a breeze, we set up the field kitchen in the shelter of trees to avoid the sun. They struck, finding parts of our anatomy that had not been bathed in repellent, and anyone who had to "use the facilities" returned to the group scratching parts of his body one usually does not touch in mixed company. It was a rapid lunch, and we soon were back on the river, vowing in the future to dine while drifting, our boats lashed together.

One member of our party was positive she had the mosquito problem solved: she had gulped one of the more obscure vitamin compounds for several days before the trip and did not bother bringing repellent, which she said gave her a skin rash anyway. The vitamins failed and she wore a plastic rainsuit, plastic kitchen gloves and a hat with netting on the entire trip, sweltering during the long, hot days, while insisting it was worth it to keep the mosquitoes from dipping into her bloodstream.

We had another serious session with them when we stopped for dinner in a pleasant grove of aspens. We were able to keep them off our bodies, but were unable to keep them from committing suicide in our beef stroganoff and cups of coffee and tea. Yukoners only shrug at the prospect of mosquitoes in their food: "Adds protein."

With tent netting, repellents and mosquito coils—the latter a smudge-pot gadget in the shape of a coil that smolders and whose smoke drives them away—the scourge can be controlled. Most towns in the Yukon are sprayed each summer and repellent is unnecessary. But it is another, sadder story for animals. Horses are especially susceptible to them—not to their bites as much as to getting them clogged in their nostrils and suffocating. Horsemen who keep them where mosquitoes are rampant, especially around bogs and marshes, must spread a salve solution in the horses' nostrils so they can keep the insects blown out. During the early days of exploration in the

99

North it wasn't unusual for horses to be killed by the mosquitoes and black flies that inhabit the tundra country above the tree line.

Mosquitoes, like geography, are a constant in the North, a part of fate to be endured. Significantly, Yukoners seldom mention them. Each spot on earth has its natural disadvantages, and during the northern summers it is the insects that keep Eden beyond reach, somewhere around some undiscovered bend.

The river above Carmacks is a maze of dead-end sloughs and islands, some of which give the eerie impression that they are moving. The swift water hits their upstream, prowlike end and splashes onto the piles of driftwood and rocks, giving the appearance of a bow wave. Then the highway appeared on a hillside and we passed beneath a powerline and the bridge at Carmacks came into view.

When the Klondike Highway between Whitehorse and Dawson City was completed in the early 1950s, the Yukon government—and most other people in the North—assumed the steamboats were as much a matter of history as the mastodon. But there were a few who felt otherwise and were outraged when the Carmacks bridge was neither built high enough for the paddlewheelers to clear nor fitted with a drawbridge mechanism. There were and are people who firmly believe the tourist industry will support an elegant paddlewheeler during the summer months, and they view the Carmacks bridge as another tiresome example of bureaucratic stupidity.

When the *Keno* was fired up for the last time in 1960 and taken down to Dawson City to become a museum, she suffered the indignity of having her top deck dismantled and the stack removed in order to clear the bridge. The old-timers, who are always accused of wanting time to stand still, detest that rather ordinary bridge because, if nothing else, it represents the arrogance of the automotive society that replaced the beloved paddlewheelers. They know the paddlewheelers are uneconomical and they know that era will never return and they know there is nothing they can do about it. But they don't have to like it.

The dominance of the automobile brought changes to

the entire North that are not always pleasant. For one thing, they meant that, for the first time in Northern history, vandalism became a fact of life. Cabins in the bush and homes in the towns had to be locked. That one fact, as much as the Carmacks bridge, gave definition to the new way. Theft, once the equal of murder, now is accepted as an irritant, and to a man who lived the first fifty years of his life without fear of mindless vandalism and casual theft, who knew he could leave his home and return a year later with everything intact—to such a man the old days and the old ways were infinitely better.

It is not so much that they resent the passing of the old ways as much as they do the passing of the old values. The old-timers do not pretend life was beautiful in their youth; events of which they speak—illness in the bush, poor food, inadequate housing and clothing—indicate otherwise. But the social order was so rigid, yet so fair, that Mounties often went for years without making an arrest. Their primary duties in the pioneer years consisted of helping people more than enforcing laws. The reports they wrote after making long patrols into the wilderness were likely to contain stories of helping trappers repair cabins, treating the sick and injured and hauling gold nuggets to the bank. The two basic laws north of the 60th Parallel—don't kill, don't steal—were the dominant social rules. But that era has gone. The highways gave mobility to the mischief makers, and their deeds now lack the personal touch of stealing from a neighbor.

It isn't limited only to the automobile travelers. In spite of the "take only photos, leave only footprints" public relations campaign that gave backpackers and paddlers such a pure image, theft and vandalism have increased in the bush. The wilderness camper who builds a campfire with boards from a cabin is as much a vandal as the one who throws rocks through windows in town.

A few years ago when the young people of the counter-culture discovered the Yukon and flocked to it by the thousands, their self-proclaimed innocence and abhorrence of violence and theft suffered as much as those who drive automobiles. They, too, had thieves in their numbers, and no old-timer will ever forget that it was a young man who in 1974 set fire to those magnificent old steamboats at Whitehorse, the *Whitehorse* and *Casca*—and that he had to climb over a high chain-link fence decorated with Keep Out signs to do so. The old people stood watching, tears in their eyes, as flames rapidly consumed those relics of their youth, feeling a deep hatred for those who burned them, those who did not care that they were burned, and those who did not severely punish the arsonist when he was caught.

In the Yukon it is not the generation gap that afflicts the old and the new ways; it is a matter of basic morality. And the bridge at Carmacks is one of the symbols of this shift in values as much as the displays of door locks in Whitehorse department stores.

Carmacks was named for its first white resident, George Washington Carmack, who, with his brother-in-law Skookum Jim and Jim's cousin, Tagish Charley, discovered the Klondike gold in 1896.

In all the words written about Carmack, very little has been said about his travels on the river, and he was a great traveler. While he made his permanent home at Carmacks, where he had a pipe organ and a fine library heavy on the sciences (especially astronomy), he constantly ranged up and down the Yukon River from Lake Bennett to Alaska, covering more than 1,000 miles a season as he visited Kate's family on the lakes, then drifted down to the Fortymile and beyond, then poled and tracked back again to Carmacks for the winter.

Carmack and the other early travelers did not have motors for their boats, and steamboats were not yet running. Their boats were heavy—too heavy to portage any distance— and they had to track upstream, only occasionally finding water slack enough to pole and paddle against. More often, one was in the boat to pole and keep it away from the bank while the other pulled, or tracked, it along.

In spite of the hard work, those first residents of the river could average 20 miles a day upstream and frequently traveled in groups of three: one tracking, another in the boat with a pole, and the third at the rear with another rope or pole to push it. When George Dawson, the hunchbacked dwarf and geologist who wrote with the style of an English novelist, traveled through the Yukon in 1887, he noted that the Indians did not rely heavily on the rivers for transportation. Instead, they preferred slinging on crude backpacks and hiking across country, sometimes traveling at right angles to the rivers.

Many of the earlier travelers did not invest their labor in boats. They became adept at building rafts with shelters on them and would drift downriver several hundred miles, then walk back if they felt compelled to return to the upper river. A few Indians built skin bull boats that appeared to the white men as disasters waiting to happen and it wasn't unusual to see an entire family, plus the dog team, loaded into a moose-hide boat drifting calmly downriver. After Dawson City became the major city in the Yukon, some travelers built large rafts and used them for both transportation and income; they floated them to the sawmill at Dawson City and sold them for lumber.

We approached Fort Selkirk late in the evening after a long day of weaving in and out of rooted trees and other debris bobbing in the high, brown water. Overhead were billowing clouds that previously had existed only in our memories of childhood, and now they were tinted with red and yellow from the low sun that sank beneath the high basalt wall across from Fort Selkirk. The wall was dark and threatening in the shadows and looked as though a Chinese emperor had ordered slaves to build it 12 miles long and 500 feet high—then lost interest and returned home. We couldn't see the buildings of Selkirk, but we saw the late amber sunlight flashing off the windows like signal fires on a remote, uncharted shore.

Fort Selkirk was built on a high bank across from the mouth of the Pelly with a ramp, dug out of the bank for steamboats, that has survived neglect, floods, and ice jams. We pulled in at the foot of the ramp and anchored the boats to rocks and wooden stakes, then settled for the night in the barnlike Taylor & Drury store, the Anglican Church, and the mission school. We set up a community kitchen in the school building because it had a functioning woodstove and chairs and desks.

Fort Selkirk is the largest ghost town in the Yukon Territory, and a middle-aged Indian couple, the Robertses, have lived there all their lives. As we already had discovered, anyone who lives alone in the bush is fair game for some of the urbanites of Whitehorse who, like many city people, cannot understand how anyone can live out of town by choice. These were the same people who had said the Brookses on Grahame Inlet were "bushed" and they also said the Robertses were simpleminded and that anyone looking for conversation would have to look elsewhere.

I wasn't surprised because an anthropologist once accused me of fictionalizing an interview with an elderly Indian woman. She would not speak into his tape recorder and he gave up in disgust, saying she could only weave baskets and live a long time. But she was willing and happy to talk about her youth that stretched back to the Indian Wars of the 1850s if one was willing to listen and not ask so confounded many questions. After the anthropologist's accusation, I wondered how many scholarly papers were written from similar stances of arrogance and asked a tribal chairman about it. He laughed and said that it is a tribal joke to tell "Indian stories" to people carrying tape recorders.

There is an assumption of superiority among most white people visiting the North, as well as other parts of the world, that gives them the inalienable right to go around poking camera lenses and tape-recorder microphones into natives' faces—"Speak, doggy, speak!" The farther north one travels the more offensive it beomes to the Indians and Eskimos, because there is a deep sense of politeness among them. One is seldom addressed by name, and frequently whole conversations will occur without a name being mentioned or one person looking at the other. It simply is not polite to be direct in this manner; one should not be put on the spot, and a direct question or statement could be interpreted as an accusation or verbal aggression.

Yet tour directors never mention this basic courtesy, and it is one reason there has been a stiffening among the original residents of the North toward outsiders. Perhaps the epitome of this superior, unfeeling attitude was reached when a Canadian sociologist went to the remote village of Old Crow to conduct experiments on the Indians (including, said one wag, feeling the bumps on their heads). The sociologist knocked on an Indian's door at three o'clock in the morning, and the moment the door opened he stuck a stethoscope or some such instrument on the Indian's chest to see how he reacted to stress. The Mounties stepped into the experiments after that and sent the sociologist away on the next plane.

With this background, we weren't expecting much of a reception from Danny Roberts at Fort Selkirk. Shortly after we arrived he came down the path that leads from his small cabin along the edge of the bank to the buildings we were occupying. He was a stocky man with Oriental features and wore forest green pants and shirt and the billed cap often adopted by motorcyclists and cab drivers. He carried a guest register and shyly, awkwardly asked each of us to sign it. He told us we could use the buildings if we took care of them and pointed out a pile of firewood for use in the schoolhouse stove and a firepit just outside.

He stood silently with us a few minutes, seldom looking into anyone's face, then walked a few paces away and stood on the bank looking across the river. That evening we established a routine we followed for the next two days, during which he told me what he wanted to tell me and, I suspected, nothing more. He would come down the path from his cabin and stand off a short distance from us, and I would walk over and stand with him, both of us gazing across the river and seldom looking at each other. Sometimes he would talk; sometimes he remained silent. But it was a comfortable silence that did not encourage talking for its own sake. Like most Yukoners living out of town, Danny was not a master of small talk and he did not dwell on abstractions. He talked about things that exist; things he could see and touch and use. He moved slowly and deliberately and saw his environment from a totally pragmatic point of view: if it works, use it; if it does not, ignore it.

He told us that he and his wife were both born at Selkirk during its heyday when there were about two hundred residents. They had gone to school in the building we were using and had never lived elsewhere for any length of time. He had worked on the Pelly River ferry before the highway bridge was built, and he cut steamboat firewood for a contract woodcutter who paid him $7 a cord.

They stayed at Selkirk because they liked the solitude and didn't feel they were far from other people. They could always take the boat up the Pelly River to visit the Bradley brothers, who farmed there. If they wanted to go to town, they could take the boat back upriver twenty miles to Minto, walk a mile to the highway, and catch a bus. But they didn't go away much because they don't care for towns. Usually he went to Pelly Crossing with the Bradleys for supplies or made arrangements with them to bring gas and oil from town for him.

Most of his job at Selkirk involved keeping tourists from walking away with everything or burning the buildings—which, like all wooden buildings in the Yukon interior, are tinder-dry and will burn with explosive speed. The government pays him a small salary as caretaker but would not provide him with firefighting equipment. During the winter he runs a trapline and keeps the snow off the Selkirk buildings with a long-handled wooden rake he built.

He said a Frenchman lived at Selkirk for a short time and brought a big Irish wolfhound with him that understood only French. Danny was teaching the Frenchman how to trap so he could get his own trapline after serving an apprenticeship of at least one year. Then he would apply for a license if he could find a trapline that wasn't being used or buy one from another trapper.

One day a fire started outside the Frenchman's cabin and when Danny tried to put it out the dog kept him away.

"The dog he didn't understand anything but French," Danny said, laughing, "and I had to go and get the Frenchman so we could put out the fire."

He took the Frenchman on the trapline with him that winter and when they came to the first trap, the dog team stopped for it to be checked. The Frenchman asked where the trap was and Danny told him "right over there." The Frenchman walked around, then stepped in the trap and sprung it harmlessly against his high boots.

"Oh, there it is," the Frenchman said, and Danny laughed harder at that story than any others he told.

Danny's daughter, Lois, came to live with them after completing high school in Whitehorse and wasn't going to leave home again. She didn't like Whitehorse or any other town, Danny said. She was nineteen that summer, a quiet, attractive girl with high, Oriental cheekbones and waist-length black hair bound in a leather thong, and she wore clean Levis and a plaid shirt. She and her mother made bead necklaces and leather purses, and she was learning to paint northern scenes on leather for wall hangings, purses and jackets.

Danny said two young men arrived at Selkirk late one summer on a flimsy raft and announced they were staying for the winter. He wasn't excited about company for the winter—especially two people who showed up without heavy parkas, a gun, or even adequate footwear; they were wearing low-cut oxfords. When he asked how they would feed themselves, they said they would set snares for animals and nets for fish, neither of which they had with them. Danny qualifies as an expert on living off the land in the Yukon and knew they wouldn't last through October.

He gave them a chunk of moose to get them started and helped them fix up a cabin, then went to town, presumably to report them to the Mounties, who spend an inordinate amount of time protecting people from their own foolishness. When Danny came back a few days later, he saw the two almost out of sight down the river on a raft made of oil drums, which they had stolen from him. Rather than chase them for the drums he let them go, glad to see them leave. He talked to a trapper later in the winter who had seen the two on the river and offered to help repair the flimsy raft to make it safe, but they refused his offer and kept going. They drifted as far as Stewart Island, where Rudi Burian showed them how to make a proper raft, and nobody has seen them since. Danny assumes they left the river, and the North, at Dawson City.

Danny adheres to the courtesy of the bush: he will help a man if he needs help and leave him alone if he refuses. He doesn't push himself on others. If they insist on doing something that borders on the suicidal, that is their business. But if they want help, it is always available.

He keeps four or five dogs chained apart behind his cabin

and said he doesn't feed them much when they're not working during the summer. He goes out occasionally to the slough near his cabin and nets pike and grayling to feed them, and smokes the rest on a rack behind his cabin for the winter when they're working. He kills two moose each fall for his family and feeds the scraps to the dogs. He used his dogs to pull his canoe up-river before he owned a motor, and he ran along behind them on the bank. When they came to a bluff where he couldn't walk beside the river, he got into the canoe with the lead dog and let the others swim around the bluff while he poled the canoe, then got back on the bank, hitched the dogs up again and started running with them pulling.

He and his wife had a small pet dog she kept on a leash so he wouldn't tangle with the sled dogs, which are always mean from hunger and jealousy. Danny subscribes to the practice of keeping dogs always a little hungry so they'll look forward to working when they get more to eat—and of keeping them hungry for affection, too. The pet dog was kept on a leash for another reason as well: so he wouldn't go after a bear, then bring the angry beast on his tail and right into the living room, which has happened too often for Yukoners to see humor in the situation.

One dog was kept inside the fenced area and had a larger kennel than the others, and Danny said she was his retired lead dog. Lead dogs always receive more affection and attention and appear to consider themselves a separate species from the work dogs, who automatically defer to the lead animal. During the winter Danny takes the old dog into the cabin to stretch out by the fire.

The next afternoon we walked through the dense under-brush up a low hill to the Indian cemetery. We had seen Indian cemeteries at Little Salmon with the distinctive spirit houses over the graves, one of which was furnished with doll furniture and toy trucks that would be prizes on the antique market. The Selkirk cemetery was the largest on the river but hadn't been cared for in decades. It was in a grove of young spruce and balsam poplar that had grown after the town was abandoned, and most decorations were leaning precariously or lying flat on the ground.

The houses were not so numerous as at other cemeteries, but each grave had been decorated with simple, yet sophisticated woodwork. Nearly all were surrounded by a fence of sorts, some only chicken wire supported by cross-pieces of wood like sieves stood on edge. Others had elaborate wooden fences with spear-shaped designs on top of the pickets. A few had tall, almost totemlike posts with designs sawed or carved into them. One had a fish on the top made of a single board with a knot for the eye and the curving grain to represent the skeleton and tail. It looked suspiciously like a Picasso.

The most impressive spirit house of all was an A-frame rather than the usual square cabin with roof and glass windows. The A-frame was made of 1 × 4s standing on end with the boards laced at the top and the tip of each carved into a blunt spear with a single barb on one side.

There are various stories about the origin of spirit houses —including one version that credits French missionaries with introducing them. This is apparently based on the custom bred of necessity among the New Orleans French who buried the dead on top of the ground because of the high water table.

But the actual credit goes to enterprising sawmill operators who were left with stacks of logs and lumber after the gold rush fizzled out at Dawson City. They were able to capitalize on the Indians' sense of ceremony, and spirit houses were the rage in Indian cemeteries for several years. New ones are seldom if ever seen today.

As a cultural footnote, an Indian cemetery that stands on a hill between Whitehorse and the airport became a popular tourist attraction and a mandatory stop for guided tours (and what the guides say about them is anyone's guess). In a fit of pride, the Whitehorse Chamber of Commerce told the Indian community that they should clean up the cemetery and paint the spirit houses, "and take a little pride in their culture." That rated a bitter laugh among Indians who didn't like tourists traipsing across their cemetery. They replied that, if the spirit houses should be painted, perhaps the Chamber of Commerce would like to do the job. And that is why the group of spirit houses overlooking Whitehorse are painted red and blue and black and brown and tan.

One can only speculate what historians will have to say about religion and the "Indian problem" when, and if, our civilization goes the way of the Romans or the Mayans. It should intrigue them to note that the dominant, or conquering, civilization was unable either to completely assimilate the vanquished into their society or to defeat them without suffering pangs of guilt that emerged generations after the deed was done. Will they condemn us for not forcing a homogenization of our society that would simply swallow up the Indians and the blacks and the Chicanos and the French-Canadians? Or will they applaud us for structuring a society with the flexibility to permit diversity and the sense of justice that allows the defeated to seek redress?

Obviously we cannot answer these questions that are being asked daily in the Yukon Territory by those who see the Indians as a culture that deserves preservation, those who resent the federal funds spent on them and those who agree with a prominent American actor who thinks they deserve nothing because they "lost the war." Yet one cannot help but be sympathetic with the first missionaries who came to the North, and the Indians whose souls were their target. There is something at once infinitely poignant and irritating about people so dedicated to their beliefs that they would subject themselves to harsh climate and inadequate diet to bring a new system of thought to a people who already had a system that worked well for them, one based on their immediate, peculiar needs.

The Indians of the Yukon interior have often been dismissed by whites because they had no intricate culture and few arts compared with the coastal tribes in Alaska and British Columbia. But those sympathetic to the Indians argue that they were a people who never had enough to eat. Their whole lives were devoted to food gathering, and there is grim evidence of frequent famines and occasional forays into cannibalism. It is significant that the Indian population (there are no Eskimos) has almost trebled since the arrival of the white man and his medical advantages. Whether the increase of any population is good for humanity as a whole is a separate question.

The impact of Western religion on the natives of the North, or any other part of the world, can only be speculated

110

about at this time, but it is known that when other branches of Christianity followed the Anglican Church to the Yukon the Indians were more likely to be confused than gratified at a choice.

One touching incident illustrated this confusion. An elderly chief and his wife appeared at a Mountie post, set up camp nearby, but were too shy to discuss the problem that obviously had brought them in from the wilderness. After the Mounties decided the chief was not going to approach them, the commanding officer went to the chief's tent and won his trust.

"This was a good man," said one of the Mounties who was there. "He had been married to the same woman for years and had five children, and we wanted to help him.

"The chief finally told us the Catholic priest had said he was living in sin because he'd never been married in church. Imagine! We asked the Anglican priest if he would be willing to perform the ceremony, and he said he would be delighted. The old man and his wife went away happy."

It is easy to condemn religion for such actions, but it is not quite that simple: missionaries, like other explorers, are representatives of the society from which they came. While all of us do what we think is right, our actions are still an extension of our intellectual and emotional environment. We cannot blame the missionaries without blaming ourselves or our ancestors.

In Fort Selkirk the Anglicans established a mission five years before the gold rush with a minister-teacher and his wife assigned there while the diocese office was still at Fortymile more than 220 miles downriver, all part of the religious empire built by the just and dedicated Bishop William Bompas. Strangely, when the town was abandoned the church did not take its records out of the school and left them, along with furniture and fixtures in the church, as though they planned to return.

While looking through the teachers' quarters we found, amid the litter on the second floor and scattered around like old leaves, several grade cards and teachers' reports on students who now have reached their middle years. They bore surnames such as Joe, Tom Tom, Luke, Blackjack, Bill, and Isaac, and one of the teachers reported to mission headquarters that "during the week of January 15, the weather was too cold to hold school (–55 F.). Since four days were lost then, and so many during the previous quarter, the half-holiday in memory of the late Governor General was not observed. There was no knowledge of the holiday until it passed in any case."

The teacher also reported that one girl "was not able to assimilate the teaching," and that another "lacked the will to learn." The others "are making the most of their opportunity."

We picked up the papers and concealed them beneath a pile of notebooks on a shelf, feeling vaguely guilty—as if we had peeked into a child's diary. We read these reports at a time when the most popular assessment of the Indian claims suits under way was that the whites used to distrust an Indian with a weapon; now they worry whenever they see one carrying a briefcase.

Not all Indians have plunged into the consumer society with its welfare programs as an alternative for those unable or unwilling to compete. Far to the north of Dawson City, almost a hundred miles beyond the Arctic Circle on the edge of the tree line and out on the tundra, remote enough to exercise control over their lives, are the Indians of Old Crow. No highway leads there, and the monotony of the maze of mudflats, ponds and sluggish streams does not encourage a tourist industry. No travel writer has returned extolling its beauty, and the thrice-weekly plane service implies a layover in a town on the very edge of civilization that has no tourist facilities, no restaurants, no motels, no guided tours and no nightlife in a land where the sun never sets all summer.

Although no legal restrictions are placed on visitors, one must by sheer necessity obtain permission to stay there overnight because the only quarters are in the school or the RCMP post. Otherwise, visitors must camp with the swarms of mosquitoes and black flies.

Old Crow is not an inviting place for drop-in guests, yet many who do visit the town strung out along the Porcupine River bank return with the feeling they have met some "real"

Indians, much the way we felt after meeting the Brookses and the Robertses—all "real" Northerners.

Sociologists and environmentalists have lived briefly in Old Crow as part of the minuscule white community—the RCMP, a teacher, the clergy and a nurse—but none have produced reports of their findings more specific, more complete, even lyrical than those filed several times a month by Edith Josie, the Old Crow correspondent for the *Whitehorse Star* since 1962.

In English written the way she speaks it, which would make a grammarian blanch but gets the message across succinctly, Miss Josie has been delighting and informing Canadian readers since her first column was printed. Fortunately, her first editor was wise enough to print the column exactly the way she wrote it, misspellings, erratic punctuation, fractured grammar and all.

Miss Josie has never married, but she has had a number of children, as women are expected to do, and reported the birth of one in this manner:

> At 8:30 P.M. I had a baby boy and he's 6lbs. Miss Edith Josie had a baby boy and I give it to Mrs. Ellen Abel to have him for his little boy. She was very glad to have him cause he's boy. I was in Nurse Station and Miss Youngs sure treat me very nice. Myself and baby I really thanks her very much for her good kindness to me.

Then she went on to other community affairs.

> Helicopter been to Old Crow and went down river to camp. When he was flying toward Old Crow they see few caribou across. Hope everybody see caribou this fall and get meat for winter and also for the dogs. Sorry nobody get moose this year. They never hunt and all they do is cutting wood for sale and also the logs for school.

She is a master of crowding a lot of information, an occasional gripe and a deep sense of place into a relatively brief column, such as one of her New Year's reports:

It is New Year Eve and everybody are excited for shooting at midnight.

Around 11 P.M. the service for 1964 and after church our Mr. Chief Charlie Peter serve coffee and cake at the hall. The next day it is 1964 and everyone happy and go around to shake hand for New Year Day.

Joe Netro sure busy with selling firecracker that day. Too bad Mr. Philip had none in his store but still he's doing better with his store. When he get stuff in his store everyone buy from him.

It is warm weather all winter some time cloudy and snow. Even no wind and sure good weather. Sure lots of timbers and wood around Old Crow, even dry willows. But still Mr. Neil McDonald got no wood for post office and when the mail plane arrived Old Crow he nearly freeze in post office when he give the mail out. He really got time to get wood but he never and when the plane is going to come with mail he sure get busy for wood but no one look at him. And he always picks up chips before plane come. And now he expects plane while that he got no wood.

If she didn't have much to say, she simply didn't say much: "At last Fort Yukon aircraft arrived Old Crow with few mail but not much."

During the winter many Old Crow men trap muskrats in the sloughs and ponds around town, which is why the town was built and maintained over the years. The migrations of the barren ground caribou bring them food and the weather controls their activities. It is little wonder that Miss Josie's columns have always been punctuated with meteorological information:

Some lake are frozen and hard for the people to set trap in the Flat and they came into town with not many rat. I hope they doing fine after no ice on the lake. It is getting lots of water and some snow is melting around town.

Sure lots of ducks but still we never see birds. We never see caribous but we might see caribous sooner.

114

A few days later that May she reported: "The water go this high —nine and a half foot rise." The next day she reported: "Five foot rise."

Soon after her columns began appearing, word spread around Canada and she became something of a celebrity. A book of her columns was printed and the *Whitehorse Star* began publishing each year's columns in softcover books. Occasionally, but not on a regular basis, she began making trips to Whitehorse and has since traveled over much of Canada. Wherever she has gone she has been treated as a celebrity and a spokesperson for life as it could be in the bush. This has obviously pleased her, but it has not changed her attitude toward Old Crow. One of her first trips to Whitehorse resulted in this mixed reaction to the territorial capital:

> I got to Whitehorse and before the supper myself and Mrs. Marsh went to the store just to see how it look. So when we went in Mrs. Marsh bought a hat for herself and I bought two scarves. Was this wonderful.
>
> When I visit the store sure lots of things to see, I really agree my trip to Whitehorse. We will go to Whitehorse Inn lunch, Mrs. Marsh and myself. Thank very much for the dinner. I went to *Whitehorse Star* visit them. They are very glad to see me and so do I. I wish I will visit them some day again cause they are very kind people. I hate to live Whitehorse but I will try and come back when *Whitehorse Star* want me to have another holiday trip.
>
> April 2 when I coming toward Whitehorse I don't expect that I will have a great time but now I really enjoy it very so much.
>
> I really interested my trip to Whitehorse and I sure do hope and get back to Old Crow safe where my home is.

In January 1969, a group of oil company representatives flew to Old Crow to explain what they would be doing the following summer around the area while searching for oil deposits.

They expect oil company and at last they arrived Old Crow on January 23 soon they arrived and the people start the meeting with oil company. [She listed them by name and company they represented.]

This are the oil company, just visit Old Crow and talk with people how they going to work in the Flat, they won't work on the lake and I don't think any animals will destroy.

But people think they going to damage the fish and rats on the lake so they make meeting soon they arrive.

They glad to meet the people and sure nice people. So I wish people should be glad that any kind of company going to work. They all should agree instead of making meeting.

Almost two months later the subject was still on Miss Josie's mind and she wrote another story, what newspapermen call a follow-up:

Last month oil company been to Old Crow and they held the meeting and disguest about Crow Flat.

We all know Charlie Abel make a good speech and every one agree what he say.

He say he been up around Whitestone with trapping good many years. He's right no matter how cold he travel and set trap every year.

Some people glad for oil company going to work for oil. Because the boys going to make good money.

In 1963, shortly after she took over the correspondence job, a large group of scientists flew to Old Crow to observe an eclipse of the sun. Miss Josie reported the event, putting it into a slightly different perspective from what most correspondents would:

Mr. Rev. J. Simon making feast with one moose. Everybody had a nice supper. They been cooking for him and later that they set table for white people and the Indians were eating on the ground by Mission. Sure everybody enjoy to eat out door. While they cook for James the sun is eclipse around 11 A.M.

Her most poignant report was written in the summer of 1967, an obituary for her mother, which should help lay to rest beliefs by some whites that Indians either conceal their emotions or that they are emotionally stunted by our standards:

My mother Elizabeth Josie pass away on August 9, 1967. She left me Edith Josie, son Amos Josie, three grandson Peter, William, Kevin. One granddaughter Jane Josie all at Old Crow. Also a son, Susie Paul and his family at Eagle, Alaska, and one son at Tacoma, Wash., U.S.A.

My Mother Elizabeth is well known in Alaska and in the Yukon and in the North West Territories. She born in 1886, in the North West Territories. She is well known by the people at Eagle, Alaska, and they will be sorry to hear of her death. She is buried at Old Crow Cemetery on August 10th at 3 P.M. Everyone attend her funeral. Many thanks to the people of Old Crow at the time of our mother death.

First of all my brother and my kids join me we will say a big thank you to Reverend Exham of Old Crow and to Reverend Simon of Fort McPherson for the wonderful Holy Communion services they hold for our mother every Sunday before her death. We will also thanks every one who pray for us.

Now to all the women white and native. Thank you for all what they donated to us for the feast we put up for our mother. And also to the men we thank them for what they gave us for the feast. Also for those who made the coffin for our mother. It was a wonderful coffin and the women made a nice cross with spruce branches all decorated with flowers.

And now to the younger people who dug the grave, they did very well and it didn't took them very long. It was raining but they never stop they kept on until they finish. On the afternoon of August 9th they dug some of it and finish the rest on the morning of August 10th.

All the women started to cook for all who work digging grave and all who work making coffin. Each one ate a meal at our place. On the morning of August 10th all the women came to our place again and start to cook for everyone in Old Crow. And all the people start to eat at noon we invited all the men first when the men finish then all the women come to eat also the kids.

Then the funeral service start at 3 P.M. When this is over close to 5 P.M. we also invited all the white people to come to the feast at 5 P.M. Nobody left out only those who can't come but they all send us a note that they can't come on account of their visitors. We also had a visitor here from Fort Yukon they are Tommy Carrall and his family. Also Doris Ward and her family. We are glad to have them here to attend the feast we put for our mother. We are really happy to have every one come to our feast. And we do hope every one have enough to eat and enjoy our feast.

My brother Amos and all my kids join me. We don't leave no one out, women white and native. And all the men and all the kids. All who help haul wood with boat for the feast. Every one of you we say a big thank you.

Old Crow is a small place and not many people but when things happen no one stay behind they are all happy and ready to help. We do [hope] this will be kept up.

Sorry we forgot to say thank you to Dick Nukon who supply plywood for the coffin. We are so happy for all what is done for our mother once more we thank every one and God bless each one of you and keep you all in good health.

We shall never forget all of you in Old Crow, for what you did for our mother. And all what you gave her to eat in her pass time. I thanks all the women who give her somethings to eat when she was in bed. Thank you. I really mist my mother but pray for us I'll be glad for that.

For once, Miss Josie did not sign off her column in her characteristic style, which has become as familiar to *Whitehorse Star* readers as Walter Cronkite's "That's the way it is" sign-off is to American audiences. Miss Josie simply writes: "This is end the news. Edith Josie."

Events appear to be catching up with Old Crow, and the days of the Indians' living off the land by hunting and trapping will soon be consigned to the realm of memories. There are serious plans to run oil or natural gas pipelines across the Old Crow Flats from the North Slope deposits in Alaska to the Mackenzie River delta to connect with the Mackenzie pipeline corridor south to the market areas (although the Council of Yukon Indians strongly oppose this). If that happens, Old Crow will change, as the once remote villages in Alaska have changed. One can foresee the time when a newspaper correspondent from Old Crow will write proper English and file proper news stories that will be lacking in both detail and personality and will represent the white man's attitude toward news rather than the natives. It will be a great loss, and a great pity.

Although former residents speak of Fort Selkirk with fondness and regret for having to leave, the air of melancholy that follows the river north like glacial silt is more pronounced there than in any other ghost town along its course. Selkirk seems abandoned rather than vacated as though the citizens were warned of a Pompeii-like disaster that did not occur. The air of melancholy is also due to the spiritual presence of Robert Campbell, one of those nineteenth-century travelers whose defeats were so spectacular that they must be considered successes of the human spirit. In the mind of many who follow careers of explorers, his last exploit in the Yukon rivals Shackleton's great failure in Antarctica. He also represented that British trait of absolute devotion to duty, no matter the odds— a characteristic lacking in American explorers, with the major exception of Meriwether Lewis and William Clark. Although Campbell did not directly represent the Crown, he was totally loyal to the Hudson's Bay Company in its crusade of profits and dominance of North America's Northwestern wilderness.

Again characteristically, he did not complain when he was unfairly turned out of the company.

Campbell was a Scottish sheep farmer attracted to Canada by an uncle who had taken a year's leave of absence from the Hudson's Bay Company to visit his family. As soon as possible, Campbell left home and went to work on the company's farm in 1830 at Red River, near present-day Winnipeg. The first four years were devoted to drudgery rather than exploring. His only excitement during this period was the job of driving a herd of sheep from Kentucky to the Red River Farm. Other than that, he considered the years wasted.

Then he was transferred to the company's post at Fort Simpson, the depot for the vast Mackenzie River drainage in the Northwest Territories where the Liard River enters the Mackenzie. He learned to grade fur rapidly by a glance and a touch, how to barter with the Indians and how to speak their jargon. His wilderness training continued under the guidance of company officials, who were paid to worship the profit motive and judged junior employees on their potential in the same field. Two years later Campbell was appointed factor of the post, and he immediately began planning an expedition into the unknown country to the northwest of Fort Simpson across the Rocky Mountains into what is now north-central British Columbia.

He made his first sojourn when one of his men, John Hutchinson, returned in the tail end of an August from the new fort he was supposed to have established on Dease Lake, far up the Liard. But the Hutchinson party went only to Fort Halkett, where the Smith River enters the Liard. There they were told a large party of Coast Indians—the company's bitter rivals for interior trade—were on their way to attack them. They dropped everything they had and ran back to Fort Simpson.

Campbell was angry, called them cowards and used the opportunity to make his first real trip into the unknown regions. He set out with a group of men, then lost most of them through desertions and had to return to the fort for more. Winter caught him at Fort Halkett, but after setting up winter quarters he marched on up the Liard to Portage Brûle, where Hutchinson's party had fled, and found the bales of goods "scattered about all the way down to the water's edge, just as they had been dropped by the men running to the canoes." Only wild animals had visited the spot since. No Indians.

Campbell's men were reassured by this information, and he had no trouble getting them to winter over, then follow him the next spring on over to Dease Lake. They spent the rest of that summer building a fort about 5 miles from the mouth of the Dease River, and Campbell left with an interpreter named Houle and two trusted Indians, Lapie and Kitza, to explore farther into the wilderness.

Their first contact with Indians came at the Tuya River, where the local Indians had built a rickety wooden bridge across a narrows called Terror Gorge. They saw an Indian standing across the bridge watching them from the doorway of his hut. While Campbell and his two Indian guides were inching their way across the bridge the Indian vanished, leaving his meal heating over a fire. Campbell noted that the food was in a metal pot, which proved the Indians were in the coastal trade zone. They took some food from the pot, left a knife and tobacco in payment and returned to the other side of the gorge to camp.

The owner of the hut returned the following day with several other Indians. The tobacco and knife served as an entrée, and the Indians crossed the bridge bearing a peace pipe. They told Campbell they were camped about 12 miles away, but that he should not go there because their tribe, the Nahanni, was ruled by a dictator who acted as middleman between the interior Indians and the Russians, who at that time controlled Alaska's coast. Campbell ignored the warning and set out for the encampment.

Before they entered the big encampment, Campbell armed himself with everything he could stick into his belt, sling over his shoulders and stuff into his pockets. The chief greeted him and produced a bottle of decent whiskey, which he passed around to Campbell's men, then invited them into his tent. The Indians outside were in a great uproar and got so rowdy that at one point they picked up the tent above the chief and visitors and moved it a few feet. The chief crawled out and informed them much blood would be spilled if Campbell's party was harmed. Then Campbell stepped outside and fired a few rounds from his portable arsenal, which further dampened their spirits.

The wilderness etiquette completed, Campbell returned to the top of a high hill they'd crossed above the camp, cut the HBC initials on a tree to take possession of the region, and raised the company flag.

Before they began the return journey, Campbell met the remarkable chieftainess of the Nahanni, a beautiful woman who said Campbell was the first white man she had ever seen.

"In her actions and personal appearance she was more like the whites than the pure Indian race," Campbell wrote. "She had a pleasing face lit up with fine intelligent eyes which when she was excited flashed like fire. She was tidy and tasteful in her dress. To her kindness and influence we owed our lives more than once," he went on. It was the stuff of a romantic novel.

He decided to return to Fort Simpson for trade goods, and the chieftainess accompanied them for a few miles for their protection and told Campbell to flee for the Terror Bridge in case some of the young bloods pursued them. They did and reached Dease Lake without incident and found the fort's construction going well. Campbell and Lapie then left for Fort Simpson in a pine-bark canoe. At Fort Halkett they changed it for one made of birchbark, and were almost swamped in Hell's Gate Rapids on the Liard.

During his travels a tight-fisted Scot named Murdock MacPherson was placed in charge and he denied Campbell's request for trading goods and provisions for his men at Dease Lake. Campbell therefore had to return empty-handed just ahead of winter and tell his men they had only starvation rations to get them through the winter. It was to be only the first of several starvation winters Campbell endured. The food supply got so low that winter that he split the party and sent some of the men back to the Liard River to shift for themselves. Those he kept with him spread out along the shores of Dease Lake, living off the land on a diet of small animals, birds, fish, lichens, skins and, finally parchment.

Their continual search for food was interrupted infrequently by parties of Indians, but toward the end of winter the chieftainess Campbell had befriended a few months earlier came by with some food.

> She ordered her servants (all leading Indians there had slaves) to cook the best they had for our use, and it was served under her directions. We partook of a sumptuous repast—the first for many a day—consisting of excellent fried salmon and delicious caribou meat. I felt painfully humiliated that I could not make a suitable return, or even send her, when she left, with a train of dogs to the south end of the lake. I could only cherish the wish in silence.

The meeting wasn't completely jovial, Campbell noted. A group of Indians rushed into the room he and A. R. McLeod, Jr., shared and—

> seized our weapons from the racks on the wall and would assuredly have shot us had not the Chieftainess, who was lodged in the other end of the house, rushed in and commanded silence. She found out the instigator of the riot, walked up, and stamping her foot on the ground, repeatedly spat in his face, her eyes blazing with anger. . . . I have seen many far-famed warrior Chiefs with their bands in every kind of mood, but never one who had such an absolute authority or was as bold and ready to exercise it as that noble woman. . . .

Historians and anthropologists have tried in vain to uncover a romance between Campbell and the woman. Under the circumstances of near starvation such an event is unlikely, since romance is usually one of the first urges to vanish when the belly is empty.

That September Campbell was ordered to explore farther into the north because the company had leased the entire Russian interior trapping grounds. He wintered at Fort Halkett and set out the following May with Houle, Lapie and Kitza, plus a fourth man, north across Dease Lake to the Liard River and up it to its source, a beautiful two-pronged lake he named Frances in honor of the wife of Governor George Simpson. They paddled to the end of the west arm, then walked over the continental divide, going without food for three days, and discovered a large river flowing northwest: "I named the bank from which we caught the first glimpse of the river 'Pelly Banks,' and the river 'Pelly' river, after our home governor, Sir H. Pelly."

They walked down to the river and "drank out of its pellucid water to her Majesty and the H.B.Co." Then, "We constructed a raft and drifted down the stream a few miles and threw in a sealed tin can with memoranda of our discovery, the date, etc., with a request to the finder to make the fact known . . . we retraced our steps to Frances Lake, highly delighted with our success."

They returned to Fort Halkett for the winter without having seen a single Indian.

Again they endured a near-starvation winter, and in the spring they returned to Fort Simpson to find that the parsimonious MacPherson had been replaced by a more generous and realistic John Lee Lewes. George Simpson, who had been knighted during Campbell's absence, wrote Campbell encouraging him to explore the river he had discovered, guessing correctly that it eventually emptied into the Pacific.

Other duties prevented Campbell from retracing his route to Frances Lake until the summer of 1842. He reached the lake on August 16 and began the construction of a trading post, the first in what was to become the Yukon Territory, at the foot of a tall stone spire they named Simpson's Tower. They had adequate food for the winter for a change, and enough trade goods for a long trip the following summer. While he and a few men worked on the trading post, others went down to Pelly Banks to put up a shanty for shelter while building a birchbark canoe from bark they had packed over from Fort Liard.

When the ice cleared the following June, the seven men entered the Pelly River in the 1,000-pound canoe and six days later entered what is now the Yukon. Campbell named the river above the Pelly intersection the Lewes, and then continued on down the big river for several miles. They came upon a band of Wood Indians who had never seen a white man before, led by a chief with the melodious name of Thin-ikik-

124

thling. He was as friendly as his name and told Campbell he should not go farther downstream because the tribes below were vicious and had cannibalistic tendencies. Reluctantly, and only because his men were frightened, Campbell turned back up-river. Three days later they met a large party of Indians, whom they had seen several miles downstream lighting signal fires on hilltops. The Indians on the bank, he wrote,

> were very hostile, standing with bows bent and arrows on the string, and would not come down from the high bank to meet us. I sent some tobacco to them to assure them of our peaceful intentions but they would scarcely remove their hands from their bows to receive it.
>
> We then ascended the bank to them, and our bold and at the same time conciliatory demeanour had the effect of cooling them down. We had an amicable inter-view with them, carried on with words and signs. It re-quired some finessing, however, to get away from them; but once in the canoes, we quickly pushed out of range of their arrows and struck obliquely downstream for the opposite bank while I faced about, gun in hand, to watch their actions.

His men were bone-weary from the hard paddling and strain of the day, so Campbell put them inside his tent that night and stayed up all night on guard, reading Hervey's *Meditations* and watching for an enemy he could not see. Months later, after he became friends with the Indians of that area, they told him they watched him all night long from the brush nearby and planned to jump him if he relaxed his vigil. They said they would have jumped him while he was drinking from the river if he had stooped over and drunk directly from the river rather than dipping water in his horn cup.

In the meantime, without Campbell's knowledge, an-other post farther north had been established by HBC employees who crossed the low range of mountains east of the Mackenzie River to the Porcupine River and drifted down it to the river Indians called the Youcan. They established Fort "Youcan" about a mile up the main river from the Porcupine mouth. It was in Russian territory, whch didn't bother the HBC management. Four years were to pass before Campbell, at the mouth of the Pelly, and W. L. Hardisty, at Fort Youcan, knew they were on the same river.

Because of the short summers and vast distances to travel to and from Canada's main centers, furs, trade goods and provisions were transported on a seven-year cycle to and from Forts Yukon and Selkirk. It took four seasons to get the material across Canada, up the Mackenzie, and across the mountains to the forts, and three years to get the fur back to the marketplace.

Campbell established Fort Selkirk in 1848 after making a trip down to Fort Yukon, and gave names to the main rivers along the way: the Stewart for a friend, J. G. Stewart; and the White for its milky color. On his arrival at Fort Yukon, he found he just missed another old friend, Alexander Hunter Murray, who had left the previous day for a way station named La Pierre's House on the upper Porcupine. Campbell caught up with him and from La Pierre's House they walked over the mountains to the Peel River and drifted it to Fort McPherson, then went south up the broad Mackenzie to Fort Simpson. After loading up with provisions, Campbell then returned to Fort Selkirk, making the great circular route of some 2,000 miles in one summer. It was only a stroll compared with what was to come four years later.

Although affairs appeared to be in order at Fort Selkirk for the next two years, the exploration, hardships and frustrations of an increasingly demanding HBC were beginning to take their toll on Campbell. Added to this was being sentenced to months in small, low-ceilinged cabins amid smelly bodies, filthy clothes, and unsanitary conditions. During the winter of 1851–1852 Campbell began brooding on his own death and wondered if he had really accomplished anything of value during the past two decades. On his forty-sixth birthday, February 22, 1852, he wrote in his diary the question: "And to what use have I made of the past year and years. . . . O how improperly I have wasted them."

Later that spring he saw a magpie chattering at his window and was convinced throughout the remainder of his life that the bird tried to communicate something to him. He prayed at the time that "God grant it may be the forerunner of good tidings."

Campbell made a fetish (for those days) of bathing every day of the year, perhaps the memory of those rancid winters back in the Rockies fresh in his memory, and in his journal told of the convenience of the fort to the river,

> which enabled me to enjoy the luxury of a bath in the river every morning. This practice I kept up until the ice got too thick. As the season advanced our cook would knock at my door and tell me the hole was made in the ice ready for me. I would then run down with a blanket round me, dip into the hole, out again and back to the house, my hair often being frozen stiff before I got there. After a good rubdown I would dress and no one who had not tried it can have any idea of the exhilirating glow produced on the whole system by this hydropathic treatment.

His arrival at Fort Selkirk had involved a bit of luck. The local Indians had recently broken off trade with the Chilkats because of the latter's superior attitude and continual rudeness while trading. Campbell arrived during a standoff when the local Indians would hide in the forest when the Chilkats appeared, leaving them frustrated. The Chilkats had yielded somewhat because they needed the trade goods, and they had to offer better terms than in the past.

Campbell worried about the Chilkats, who made annual treks over what would later become the Dalton Trail from Haines Inlet down to the Fort Selkirk area, and over Chilkoot Pass and down the river. But no unpleasant situations occurred during the first three years of the fort's existence, although their annual visits continued and their resentment was obvious. Taking into consideration the remoteness of the post, life wasn't too bad. They found adequate game and fish, and Campbell had brought a milk cow up from Fort Yukon.

Anthropologists traveling through the Yukon in later years were convinced Campbell had taken an Indian wife, who bore him children. Although this was never mentioned in his journals or the book he wrote based on the journals, it is possible he did so and kept the information from the HBC, since they frowned on their leaders becoming attached to one place, and Simpson had admonished Campbell to stay single. It is known the Indians considered Campbell a shaman, and he encouraged this belief by telling the Indians he was immune to bullets. The belief was enforced with the medicine he carried to treat his staff and friendly Indians; indeed, on one occasion he resuscitated an Indian boy who almost drowned.

The post grew to include at least fourteen white families, plus several Indian families, whom Campbell hired as hunters and laborers. Life there settled comfortably into a routine.

Toward the end of July 1852 Campbell sent most of his staff out on trips trading and hunting, which left only himself and four white men at the post. Three weeks later, on August 20, a band of twenty-seven Chilkats arrived while Campbell and his men were outside the post cutting hay for the cow. They saw the Chilkats coming and hurried inside the post and met them there. One of the Chilkats showed Campbell a letter from the commander of the HBC's tiny steamboat *Beaver*, saying they had been reprimanded for their rude behavior at Fort Selkirk the previous summer and that they had promised the commander they would be less troublesome in the future. Campbell was very uneasy and believed their showing the letter could also be interpreted as a threat: "Though their turbulence occasionally subsided into partial quiet, it was like a volcano, ever ready to burst anew. They were never for a moment out of mischief, and it defied our vigilance to watch them in every corner of our premises.

> The two wives [of two white men] who were in the kitchen made off for the woods, and soon after were followed by one of the men, events of which I was not aware for several hours after, and as it diminished our force, it increased the audacity of these villains. In the afternoon of the next day (August 21), a boat not expected until the close of October, with two canoes, was hailed coming down the Pelly, in which, as it fortunately happened, were two of the hunters and their families.

This aroused their fury, and as the boat neared, the Chilkats rushed out with their guns and knives, though ignorant who or how many were in the boat. Having yet some control over them, I left McLeod to notice the house and to prevent bloodshed, rushed to the bank.

The boat was passing some distance out. The Indians sprang into the water and dragged it ashore, and amidst roaring and yelling had it emptied of everything, and the two Indians disarmed of their guns, knives and axes in a moment. One of the principal leaders, "Mustash the Postman," who appeared in no way excited, with several others seized hold of one of the hunter's guns, on which I laid hold of it, and with him (each holding the gun) I approached the hall door determined to stake all for them.

An instantaneous rush was made upon me, with their guns and knives. Others seized me by the arms. Two of the guns snapped [misfired]. One Indian as he sprang at me with a knife, ripped up the side of a dog that came across him, and the blood off the blade crimsoned my arms as I evaded the blow. In one of the guns aimed at me (a brass blunderbuss) I saw four bullets but a little before the fray began. My pistols, which were concealed in my belt, were wrenched from me before I could fire; in fact, an attempt to do so would have been in vain, and all could have ended only in the indiscriminate murder of all.

There are two versions of what happened next: that of Campbell's letter to his superiors, and that of local Indians handed down through two generations of oral history and recorded long after the fact by anthropologists.

First, Campbell's version:

> They were already masters. On seeing it likely to come to the worst, I called out to our Indians to try for the store, where guns were ready for the enemy's reception, but in this sudden onset I found myself alone and could see none of our people. My attempt to gain the store was defeated; I was dragged and pushed toward

the bank, one only of those holding my arms warded off several knife thrusts, and I believe under Providence I owe my life to so many having hold of me, as those with the guns, though jumping round and round me, could hardly cover me alone.

In the struggle I felt sure of death, and it was with thankful surprise, though stunned with vexation, that I found myself released on the bank of the river, and only one of our hunters to be seen. He was out in the middle of the stream in a small canoe. Soon after, McLeod joined us. He could not get out to aid me in the scuffle. They had an axe, guns and knives at his head. He had effected his escape by a back door.

Campbell went on to explain that the others, including those who had fled to the woods, joined them downstream. They returned to the post late the next day and found the Chilkats had left after destroying everything they could and stealing what was of value. "Cassettes, dressing cases, writing desks, kegs and musical instruments were smashed into a thousand atoms and the house and store strewed with the wreck."

The Indians' version is different. They claim that Campbell was tied hand and foot and set adrift in a canoe. When a friendly Indian found him later and released him, Campbell was supposed to have said: "Have you any kind of name? Well, I am going to give you my name. Your name is Robert Campbell from now on." There is no way of proving either version is true, despite the fact that numerous Indians in that area adopted the Campbell name and still use it, just as there is no way of proving he took an Indian wife, as many single white men did under those circumstances.

But what lends a degree of credence to the hasty departure from Selkirk is a clue in what anthropologists often call the "numskull" stories interior Indians tell, with themselves or their relatives the butt of the story.

An example is the Tagish story about two young men who spent all day boiling beans they had stolen from a prospector only to find they were coffee beans. Or the Tlingit who laughed about his father-in-law, who bought a fifty-pound sack of flour from a trader, then carried it on his trapline an entire season, unopened, because he had forgotten to ask the trader what to do with it. Many Indian stories are of this nature, and those showing themselves or friends in favorable or flattering situations are rare.

With this in mind, one must consider that there is only one story handed down by the Indians in the Fort Selkirk area that presents an Indian in a favorable light, even heroic if you prefer: the story about the Indian who saved Campbell's life.

The factor at Fort Yukon would not give Campbell the support he needed to return to Selkirk, take revenge on the Chilkats and replenish the fort; such an action had to be approved by a higher authority. Even though it was early winter by the time Campbell assembled his staff at Fort Yukon, he struck out for that higher authority.

He and two men went by canoe back upriver to the Pelly and retraced the now familiar route to Fort Simpson, a 1,200-mile journey that put them in the fort by October, and they had to navigate between drifting floes of ice the last several days. He was denied permission to rebuild by officials there, too, so a month later, at the end of November, he struck out again on the frozen Mackenzie with a dog team and went upriver to Great Slave Lake and arrived at Fort Chipewyan on Christmas Day.

A day or two after New Year's, 1853, he started out again and arrived at Fort Garry on February 23, stopped a few days to rest and visit with old friends he hadn't seen in several years, then mushed on to Crow Wing, Minnesota. There he sent the men and dog teams back to Fort Garry and caught a ride in a wagon to St. Paul. Then, by steamer and train, he went to Chicago and Buffalo and finally arrived in Montreal that March. Since the previous August, then, Campbell had traveled nearly 10,000 miles, and 3,000 miles of that had been on snowshoes—a record unparalleled in northern history.

It was an exercise in futility. The company refused to give him permission to rebuild Selkirk, and he never returned to the Yukon. He took a year's leave and returned to Scotland, where he married, then returned to Canada. The company gave him a promotion to chief trader in the Athabasca district, where he established a brilliant profit record. He served with equal distinction at other posts and returned to Scotland with his wife and three children on another leave. While there, his wife died of typhoid.

He returned to Fort Garry in late 1871, brooding over his wife's death and wondering if it could have been avoided had he heeded the magpie's communication that spring morning back in the wilderness. Soon after he returned to duty, he was summoned to the Chief Commissioner's office and told he was fired for failing to observe the company's rigid policies. It seems he had transported some furs through the United States to get them to the market that season, thus avoiding a bottleneck that had developed in the normal route.

He accepted the dismissal stoically, although his friends believed the order could have easily been rescinded had he protested. He took up cattle ranching in Manitoba, and photographs in his later years showed him with an Old Testament beard gazing wearily into the camera. Campbell was only moderately successful at ranching. His heart was never in it.

The charred timbers of Fort Selkirk were soon covered by fireweed and native grasses and lay covered until the 1890s, when the missionaries arrived. Today nobody knows exactly where any of the buildings stood, but it is believed Campbell built it first on the peninsula between the two rivers, then moved to the high bank where the town now stands to avoid flooding.

The last evening we were at Selkirk, Danny walked down from his cabin and stopped, as he always did, about 100 feet from the center of activity and stood politely looking across the river, there to talk if we wanted to talk, but not forcing the issue. I walked over and chatted a few minutes, then asked if I could take a photo of him.

"Sure," Danny said, "let's go up by my boat. I'm going to run up to the farm."

We walked to the boat tied at the bank below his cabin, and he went to the cabin and returned with a jacket and rifle.

"Think anybody would want to go with me?" he asked. I immediately accepted the oblique invitation, although we hadn't had dinner. I let him get in the boat first, then took some photos of him working on the ancient motor before starting it. "Some people send me pictures," he said, and I promised I would send one after we returned home.

When he got the motor started, I untied the line and jumped into the long, narrow, flat-bottomed boat and asked him to drift down past where we were camped so I could tell them where we were going. He let the motor idle until we were even with the camp, then gunned it to hold it stationary in the swift water. I told my wife where we were going but couldn't hear her reply, and she finally shrugged and waved us on.

We crossed the Yukon and swung close to the bank on the Pelly and soon were in the cold shade of the high basalt palisade that follows the Pelly a mile or two. He kept watch on the bank for game, ignoring an industrious beaver working in the elegant poplar grove along the muddy bank, apparently intent on damming the Pelly. I began shivering and zipped up my light parka while watching the play of sun on the higher, rounded mountains to the south and the thunderhead that appeared heading our way from the St. Elias Range far to the southwest. Then we were back in the sun again, and I unzipped the parka in the sudden heat. The riverbanks fell back on both sides and a large clearing opened on the north bank. Through a screen of trees we saw two men working in the field, one driving a tractor and the other on a machine that chopped silage. We pulled in at the floating dock anchored to piling, tied up, and went ashore. There was nobody in sight, and the only sound came from the droning diesel generator in a small building with a light bulb outside to warn the men if the generator shut off.

There were several buildings of various sizes and stages of repair, a maze of rail and board fences, and close to the river was an unobtrusive peeled-log house with a dull red roof. On one side of it was a large vegetable garden, and all around the house were flowers. We saw several head of cattle out in the pasture and rows of antique farm implements behind the barn arrayed with some semblance of order, something like a museum. The wall of the generator building was covered with equipment: wheels, gears, hoses, cables, tools and a bear trap almost as tall as a man.

We stood slapping mosquitoes and waiting for the Bradleys to come in for the night. I rubbed repellent on my face and neck and offered the bottle to Danny. He waved it away and let the mosquitoes fog around his face, infrequently reaching up slowly to pluck off one that had dipped into his bloodstream.

The brothers completed the round, shut off the tractor and walked slowly across the field to us. They grinned easily and introduced themselves—"I'm Dick and he's Hugh"—and invited us into the house away from the mosquitoes. Their house was spartan, yet comfortable; unpainted and undecorated walls made it resemble a lodge more than a house. Over in one corner was a collection of instruments, including a short-wave radio, and Hugh explained it was the weather station they operate for the government, calling in daily reports to Whitehorse. Dick busied himself in the kitchen, heating water for tea.

Several rifles hung from pegs near the outer door, and a bookcase occupied one corner with a wide variety of subjects represented, from popular novels to scientific journals. The furniture was old but utilitarian and designed for comfort. From their living-room windows they could look across the Pelly River, and from the kitchen they could see the garden and their flat fields that run to the low wooded hills behind.

They said they bought the farm in 1954, and it had been in operation since 1903. They showed us a photograph taken of the farm and its original owners shortly after the land was cleared and crops planted. The unsmiling people were dressed in homespun woolen clothing, and the women wore ankle-length skirts and bonnets that gave the scene an Old Dutch atmosphere. The first owners had raised hay crops to feed the horses used each winter on the Whitehorse-to-Dawson stage road, in addition to the vegetables and beef they sold to the Dawson City market.

The Bradleys are from Lacombe, Alberta, and went through agricultural schools before they bought the farm. When Dick was twenty-four and Hugh twenty-two, they drove six head of cattle on foot down the trail from the highway at Pelly Crossing, 32 miles away. The herd was gradually increased to about fifty head. They butcher each October and sell quarters to local people and stores in Whitehorse and Dawson City. They also sell eggs from a flock of about 100 hens and try to raise 30 tons of potatoes each year.

They have a growing season of about ninety days, of which they can only hope most will be frost-free. But their records show those days run anywhere from only twenty-three to ninety-seven days a year. They told us of the killing frosts they have nearly every year, and they spoke easily and without self-pity of the years they had virtually no crop at all because of freezing weather or no rain or too much rain.

"There've been times when we think it will be our last year," Dick said, "but we always manage to pull through."

The Bradleys grow all their own meat and vegetables and grind their own flour from wheat they harvest each summer. They also have a sawmill and a device they rigged up that will split their firewood. They once lived for three years without going to town—totally self-sufficient—and the government has given them an old grader to keep their road to Pelly Crossing open.

By normal standards the Bradleys have had an incredibly rough time trying to farm at a latitude that is hostile to it. They appear to be satisfied earning enough money to buy necessities, while devoting a great deal of their energies to experimental crops in cooperation with universities in Canada. They always have several small experimental crops growing in an effort to find species and varieties that will survive the savage climate.

Federal government reports on the land north of the 60th Parallel do not offer much hope for establishing an agricultural base for the Yukon and Northwest Territories, and many observers believe both will remain territories for decades to come because they are so dependent on outside sources for basics. The mainstays of the economy—mining and tourism—are unlikely to change. The climate is too harsh to permit marketable timber, except in small areas in southeastern Yukon, and the climate is too dry for soil to be built up by decaying leaves, evergreen needles and fallen trees. Most of the good soil was scraped away during the Ice Ages, and the soil-making processes have slowed to a near halt by the combination of short summers, dry climate and the periodic fires that sweep through the scrub timber.

One suspects the Bradleys have stayed there for the challenge of finding crops that will grow and simply because they love the isolation. I asked them about problems with cattle in the severe winters, and Dick bridled at the question: "Back in the Great Plains is where it gets cold, and you hear of cattle freezing every winter there. Not here, though. It is the wind that gets them, but we have no wind when it is really cold up here. The morning it was seventy-six below zero, the cattle were lined up on the river bank waiting for us to break the ice."

While we were talking and drinking tea, a short, wiry, intense man dressed in cowboy clothes came to the door carrying an armload of books. The Bradleys introduced him simply as Larry. He said he was rafting a few head of horses down to the Yukon from Pelly Crossing and was going to keep them at Coffee Creek. They nodded and the conversation turned to books, many of which Larry had autographed by the authors. He left an armload, took several from the Bradleys' library and left.

When Danny and I prepared to leave, the Bradleys asked me to sign their guestbook. When I asked the date, they told me and we joked about it being my birthday. Danny bought a can of oil for his outboard from them and, laughing, held up the bear trap that was almost as tall as he. The Bradleys said they seldom had to use it, but occasionally a grizzly will start hanging around—and out comes the trap.

"Be sure and show him where the old winter road crossed the Pelly," Hugh reminded Danny, and we cast off and drifted down toward the Yukon in the broad, silent river.

When we returned to Selkirk, I walked down to the schoolhouse to see if any dinner had been left, and warmed the leftover stroganoff on a campstove. Slowly, one by one, the rest of the group gathered around me and watched me eat, which soon became nerve-wracking. Knowing my moods, my-wife uncovered a pan upon which rested a cake with a thick camp candle in the middle.

"Happy birthday," they said, then sang off-key. I was pleased and embarrassed by the irritation I'd felt a moment earlier. Then one of the women presented me with a small, soft package with a note wishing me a happy birthday from the Roberts family. I opened it and found a strip of tanned moose skin with a painting of a moose in browns and blues.

The next morning we walked up to the Robertses' cabin, where Danny was tending the smoldering fire beneath the fish rack. He stood away from us until I was through thanking them for the gift; then, with the emotional part of the visit done with, he came over to chat.

We had the boats loaded and were making one last check for anything we might have lost and cleaning up the litter when Danny came down to see us off. When I told him good-bye, he only nodded and looked out over the river. I saw him standing on the bank until we were out of sight.

The Klondike

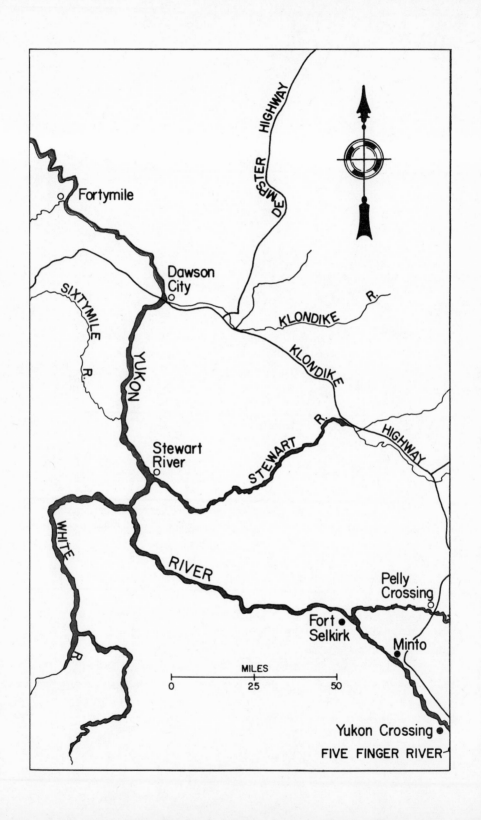

The Yukon loses even more of its intimacy after it picks up the Pelly and continues its silent rush northward beneath the basalt palisade on the east shore. The basalt is black, sometimes stained by mineral-rich streams that plummet over during spring thaw. A fringe of balsam poplar lines the edge of the cliffs, and swallows and bald eagles nest in crevices. Then it ends abruptly 12 miles downstream and the east bank almost duplicates the west with grass and low willows growing to the water's edge.

Selkirk marks a division in topography: the end of the low, undulating hills and broad, mosquito-infested banks. Most of the river north of Selkirk flows through canyon country and sometimes passes stark, barren cliffs; and there always are steep, high hills rising out of the brown, silent water. The channel still wanders back and forth along the floor of the canyon, but the canyon itself is narrower and more defined.

The river below looks more mature and established. The sweepers and cutbanks that constitute the river's signature above are not so prevalent. There are still sandbars to run aground on and a few deadend sloughs to keep boaters alert, but one gets the impression it is now the major river statistics claim it is.

Shortly after we left Fort Selkirk, the combination of too little sleep, the silence of the river and a hot sun made me suddenly very sleepy, and I stretched out on the cargo bags for a nap, after giving instructions to wake me if something interesting appeared. But it wasn't the touch of a hand or the sound of a human voice that woke me. It was the sound of dogs barking. When I awoke, all I could see was the sky above, which was not moving. The motor was silent. I was alone on the boat and back in the timber I could hear dogs.

I climbed the bank, completely disoriented, thinking that the river was flowing south and that I was walking the same direction on the sparse trail that led through wild roses and willows into a grove of balsam poplar and scrawny spruce. Then the timber opened into a clearing with two or three tired buildings. Pressed against one of them—perhaps spread-eagled would be a better word—was the rest of my party, including my wife and children. Prancing back and forth in front of them was a stocky stallion with mud splattered on his shaggy brown coat. He nickered ominously a few times, then suddenly turned and galloped across the clearing and into the timber on the far side. The dogs kept up their frantic barking and yipping, straining and lunging against their chains. Nobody spoke. I wasn't certain I was awake.

Before I had a chance to speak, an apparition appeared from the far side of the clearing that even those fully awake found hard to believe. A team of sweating, galloping horses emerged, manes flying and froth dripping from their mouths. They were pulling a skid upon which was a man, yelling, slapping them with the reins, knees bent and the wind whipping the brim of his tall-peaked cowboy hat. Running beside the team and skid was a small, excited dog and the stallion.

The team and driver swung in a wide circle in front of us, looking like a lost, demented racer from *Ben Hur* whose wheels had been lobbed off, and continued the long arc down to a building on our right. There the driver leaned his whole weight into the reins, standing the horses on their haunches. They regained their footing and stood trembling and dancing, their harness rattling like prayer wheels. The driver leaped off the skid, picked up a lard can lid and sailed it at the yipping mongrel, which tucked its tail and frantically, silently ran off into the timber.

The scene was surrealistic and unexpected as an aborigine in Alberta. None of us spoke or moved until the lard can lid flew through the air and the driver uttered his first words: "Get out of here, you noisy son of a bitch!"

I suggested quietly that we, a gaggle of tourists, leave too and led the way back to the trail toward the boats, more anxious to leave the scene than understand it. We were close to the boats when we heard someone crashing through the willows and roses toward us. We turned, suppressing the impulse to run, and then I recognized the Ben Hur. It was Larry, the cowboy I'd met the previous night at the Bradleys'.

142

"I didn't mean to spook you back there," he said, and lifted his hat to wipe the sweat off his face with a shirt-sleeve, a relaxed and casual gesture that put us at ease.

"No," I assured him. "We were somewhere we didn't belong."

"No problem," he shrugged.

We chatted briefly and he said he was from Williams Lake, B.C., and had been a rodeo rider until he got busted up too bad to ride in competition. I told him a friend's wife was from there, but before I could give her name, he said he probably wouldn't know her because he didn't know many girls—but if I mentioned the name of a horse he'd know it for sure.

The children, recovered from the series of frights, began asking questions:

"Do you trap?"

"Some."

"Make much money at it?"

"Enough."

"Those are sure pretty dogs."

"I've seen better."

"Are they mean?"

"Some are."

Abruptly he turned, said, "See you," and walked swiftly back toward the clearing, the visit ended. We stood uneasily a few moments, looking at each other and down the trail where he had disappeared, like a rare, elusive creature W. H. Hudson would have written about had he gone north.

I've often pondered that interlude and have seen Larry a few times since. He has never appeared anxious to talk to me, and I haven't pressed the issue. I still do not know why he was taking a raft of horses down to Coffee Creek early in the summer rather than to a town where they would be of use for pack trips. I've asked other Yukoners and they only shrug disinterestedly. People do those things, one told me, and who are we to wonder? It is a small but significant freedom offered by the bush, to raft horses into the middle of nowhere or to wander all summer alone or to hole up all winter reading Ayn Rand.

While the recreational traffic increases each year on the river, the population remains very small outside the towns—fewer than a dozen families in a 460-mile stretch that once had several hundred. Some predict the bush population will increase, but most doubt anyone other than summer residents will ever live on the lower river again because there is no way to support themselves. A few of the old roadhouses at the mouths of creeks are privately owned, and there is always the hope among the owners that they can restore them and rent out rooms or otherwise serve the growing boating population. It appears unlikely, unless the plans to place a steamboat back on the river to haul tourists materialize. Recreational boaters who run the river prefer sleeping in the wilderness and the sense of discovery that comes from finding an abandoned woodcutter's camp or a roadhouse.

The only business establishment that has remained in operation since the steamboat days is a modest little store on Stewart Island, operated by the Burian family. There was a small gold rush on the Stewart River at about the same time as the Klondike rush, and Jack London was one of the stampeders to winter over on the Stewart. Like most miners, he made little money that winter. The Stewart remained an important transportation corridor, however, because steamboats hauled ore out of the Keno Hill mine upriver, which produced silver, lead, zinc and cadmium. Stewart Island was a barge terminal and the store there was operated by several people until it passed into the Burians' ownership several decades ago.

We saw the sun glinting off the corrugated metal roof of the Burians' buildings when we were far upstream, and we swung the boats across the broad river for a landing. As we neared the island we saw a cluster of buildings set against the timber with a wide, green lawn that ended abruptly at the water's edge. Two or three boats were tied to the bank, one about 30 feet long with a wooden canopy and open sides. We heard the friendly yapping of dogs before we could see them, and a small group of people were walking slowly to the bank to greet us.

We drifted past the boats and beneath the high bank at the lawn's edge, turned into the current and gunned the motor to hold the boat stationary against the surprisingly swift current. When I jumped out to tie up, I looked above me and saw a cluster of bumps hanging down over my head. I pulled one loose and found a potato in my hand. Others dangled along the bank and I was filled with an uneasy wonderment: another Coffee Creek? Is this a common way to grow vegetables in the Yukon?

A small, wiry man with uncombed gray hair put my mind at ease. "The damned river took another forty feet off the island this spring, and it took half our garden with it," said Rudi Burian. "We had to hitch the tractor to that building over there and pull it away from the bank or we would have lost it too." He pointed at a building placed on large logs like a houseboat.

Their lawn covered about an acre and had been freshly mowed. The Burians and a guest, Lois Keating, had been sitting on lawn chairs listening to the radio and talking when they heard us coming down the river. Their house was larger than most we'd seen on the river, freshly painted white, and across from it was the small store with a distinctive sign, BURIAN's STORE, above the front door. Several other small buildings were scattered back in the timber, and off behind the house were three small log cabins in a neat row with a screen of trees and bushes between each. A boardwalk led from the house and store back to a square frame house with store plate-glass windows and a MUSEUM sign on it. Near it was the largest stack of firewood I'd ever seen. It was at least 8 feet high and stretched back into the timber and kept going. When we went back to look at the museum, we saw that the woodpile was a holdover from the steamboat era because the sticks were 4 feet long. I asked about it, and Rudi said he had a woodcutting contract with the steamboat company when he was a young man and had become used to having a lot of wood around.

"How much do you keep on hand at a time?" I asked.

"Two hundred cords or so," he replied.

Yvonne opened the store for us, and we loaded up on candy bars and cold drinks. There was very little else on the shelves.

"We stock it as a convenience," Rudi explained, then

apologized for charging 35 cents for a candy bar and 50 cents for a can of cola because he had to haul it 70 miles upriver from Dawson City.

Our pockets and hands full of calories, we joined the Burians in lawn chairs outside the kitchen door while the children went over to the dogs to give them the attention they had been demanding.

Rudi said the whole family goes out on traplines during the winter, and that they use line cabins for shelter. In the summer he hauls a little freight in the big boat we'd seen, but not enough to make a living at it. They operated a combination farm and ranch up the Stewart River for several years, and their oldest son, Robin, operates a gold mine up there now. When they gave up on the farm-ranch, they brought the cattle and horses down to the island.

"We had one mare in the bunch that was nearly wild, it had been so long since she'd been worked," Rudi said. "We tried to get her in the barn when winter came but she was too wild. I was afraid she'd freeze to death—should have known better—and when it dropped down to fifty below, I went out to drive her in. She wouldn't go."

Yvonne laughed at the memory. "There was Rudi out there freezing and getting madder and madder."

"Finally I said the hell with her and gave up," Rudi continued, carefully building a flat cigarette. "The next summer when the flies and mosquitoes got bad, I saw her run into the barn to get away from them and remembered all the trouble she'd caused that winter. Made me mad all over again, and I went out to the barn and drove her outside."

He keeps an ancient Chevrolet flatbed truck on the island, which they'd used on the ranch upriver. He said people started stealing his equipment and he almost caught one thief using a government helicopter to steal antiques. They had even hooked onto his disk plow but gave up on it. He laughed about the truck being there and said he drove it on about a half mile of trail on the island.

"But we're losing the whole island to the river," he said. "We'll just keep moving back into the timber, I guess."

"It is a little frightening to go to bed at night and listen to the river carving the island," Lois Keating said. "You just lay there and listen to it plop into the water."

He took us back to the row of trim cabins and said they were for rent at $2.50 per person a night, bedding not included. The cabins were furnished with handsome wood stoves, one of which could only be described as elegant, and other furniture he had picked up along the river system.

"Which do you like best?" he asked. "The one with the plywood walls or the others with logs?"

The vote was unanimously in favor of the rustic log walls, and he grumbled that he might have known: "I had that plywood shipped in to Dawson, then I brought it down here. Cost a fortune, and I'm the only one who likes it."

The Burians seem to be continually afflicted with people showing up on the island in trouble—always newcomers out to conquer the wilderness with more enthusiasm than wisdom. One group of about a dozen came down the river on a raft that kept falling apart. A girl and boy from the group came to their door and said their raft was aground and breaking up on the upper end of the island, and could the Burians help them? The Burians took them inside to dry them and warm them, and Rudi went up to help them lash it together properly. When they left, the girl said she was going back Outside to get a job and would save all her money to help the others live in the Yukon. Yvonne rolled her eyes at the thought.

They are continually amazed at the total ignorance of newcomers, she said, who are intent on living in the Yukon but almost never have adequate clothing, any idea of how they will earn a living or any skills that can be put to practical use. Like other old-timers up there, the Burians frequently utter what might be called the Law of the Yukon: You cannot live off the land. If the original Indians could not live without frequent bouts of starvation, why should it be easier for novices? Tenderfeet? *Cheechakos?*

The only newcomers who can make a success of the Yukon bush are those who work in town at least part of the time to earn enough for basic necessities, such as food and clothing. Lucky, indeed, are those who get a good trapline. They said they knew of two couples from Outside who might make it; a couple about forty miles downriver living in a trapper's cabin and working for him in the winter, and another young couple living near Dawson City who had arrived from downtown New York City, of all places, but seemed to be sensible kids. Both, the Burians emphasized, earned small incomes, raised their own vegetables and were not trying to live off moose, caribou, fish and love.

They asked us to stay overnight on the island, but we had to keep going. They said nothing, but we assumed they categorized us as typical Outsiders who lived by the clock rather than the seasons and were too hurried to enjoy ourselves.

The next morning, our last day on the river, we swung close to one shore to look at rock formations standing starkly at the edge of the river, when suddenly someone said they saw a man waving wildly on the bank. Expecting an emergency, we pulled over and beached the boats in a small protected slough with soft, muddy banks and were helped ashore by a tall young man with floppy wide-brimmed hat, long beard and wire-rimmed glasses who said he heard our motors and wanted some company.

He introduced himself as Pete and invited us back to the cabin where his wife, Mary, was already heating water for tea. We single-filed behind him through the woods and entered a small clearing where a large hothouse covered with clear plastic stood at one end of a vegetable garden. At the other end, against the edge of the dense timber, was a low, trim log cabin from which burst the sound of Neil Young singing poignant, if self-pitying ballads. The music was turned down, and soon a fair-skinned girl wearing a serape and floppy hat came out and introduced herself as Mary.

They were delighted at having company, and Pete said he sometimes listened for boat motors when the loneliness got to them. Back of the cabin were five or six beautiful huskies. The children were assured the dogs were friendly, and almost immediately the anxious animals were draped with small bodies and baby talk.

Pete said they were originally from Ohio, but moved to Berkeley, California, for school, then left there for the Yukon.

148

He worked briefly in a mine but could not stand the darkness, the foul air and the danger of lung disease. After they saved some money, they went over to Johnson's Crossing, southeast of Whitehorse, enlisted the help of a local man, built a large, sturdy raft with a shelter and sweeps fore and aft and launched it in the Teslin River.

"We picked up a fellow on the river who traveled with us," Mary said. "The sweeps were too heavy for me to operate. It took us a month to float the Teslin and the Yukon to Dawson City."

"It was the most pleasant month of my life," she said wistfully.

After they landed in Dawson City, they met Roger Mendelsohn, who trapped in the winter and worked on a tour boat in the summer. They made arrangements with him to live in his cabin and take care of his dogs in the summer, and in the winter Pete would help him with the trapline and learn the trade. He hoped to have a license and his own trapline within two years.

They started the garden in late May, built the greenhouse for tomatoes, and had been very busy carrying water from the small creek below the cabin to irrigate the garden. They had dug up old bottles from the dump near the cabin, and Pete was planning to brew beer. He also planned to build an outdoor kitchen for Mary so she could cook outside away from the cabin gloom and have a better arrangement for baking.

They said they looked forward to winter because everything slows down then and life becomes more basic and simple. Mary was working on a big project: weaving a sleeping bag for Pete made of the huskies' hair. She didn't know if it would work, but the previous winter Pete's down bag got wet and he almost froze to death.

Pete wasn't at all interested in using a snowmobile on the trapline, or anywhere else. "Dogs are the only way to go," he said. "I know a trapper who almost died because his snowmobile konked out on him in the bush, and he almost didn't make it back. He left it where it was and hasn't seen it since. Dogs will help keep you warm if you get into trouble, and you can always kill and eat them."

Mary shuddered at that, and the children howled in protest. She said she didn't believe in killing things, even mosquitoes; she simply brushes them off when they attack: "They have as much right to live as we do." They did not discuss the business of trapping animals and killing them, and we sensed it was a delicate subject between them.

She took us on a tour of the neat, clean and typically dark cabin. *The Whole Earth Catalog* was prominently displayed on the table, and she said, with a touch of reverence, that it was their bible. The tape deck was on the shelf with speakers at opposite ends of one wall, and she said Pete built a windmill power plant to charge the batteries and provide power when there was a breeze. Their tape library was large and ran heavily to rock with several albums by both Neils of the rock industry: Young and Diamond.

We left after a cup of tea made from herbs she collected and hung to dry on the porch. They seemed satisfied with a visit from Outside, no matter how brief, and did not urge us to stay longer. They asked no questions about news events in the United States, and we suspected they did not care about anything beyond their immediate lives. Rather, they seemed to have divorced themselves from anything that did not directly affect them. Since they were working so hard at establishing themselves in the wilderness, it did not appear that they were escaping anything. They had simply chosen a different way of life and seemed content, if lonely at times.

We talked briefly with another couple living near Dawson City who had chosen the Yukon way of life after spending their entire lives in the center of New York City. Their name was Russo. They went to the Yukon one summer for a vacation, liked it, and decided to stay, although they knew absolutely nothing about life outside of a city. They arranged with the Indians of Dawson City to stay in a cabin at the ghost town of Moosehide, 4 miles downriver. They moved in late in the summer, made the necessary repairs to insulate the cabin, chopped wood, fished, bought provisions to get them through the winter and arranged with a packer to care for his horses until summer for a modest income. Before 1897 Moosehide was the major Indian settlement in the area, and the busy

Bishop Bompas built a church, school, and teachers' quarters there. Gradually, over a period of fifty years, the Indians moved to Dawson City. As each log cabin was abandoned in Moosehide, the other families would demolish it for firewood until there were only half a dozen cabins left standing. The church and school were closed, but all the furniture, including a pump organ in the church and sewing machine in the teachers' quarters, was left behind. Vandals and weather took their toll on the buildings, but the Russos made repairs and covered the missing windows with plastic so the furniture remained usable and most of the keys on the organ still functioned, though they were a little off-key.

The people in Dawson City expected the Russos to last until the first cold day of October, but they stayed on, going upriver to town only for necessities and avoiding the bars and other winter diversions. They were friendly to everyone, but were devoted to each other and very serious about the new life they'd chosen.

After two winters in Moosehide, some of the Indians complained about whites living in their old village. Rather than get into an argument, the Russos began looking for another place to live. They were told about an abandoned farming community just upstream from Dawson City and found they could live there with no permission required. They moved, then received complaints from Indians that they were abandoning Moosehide and nobody would be there to protect it. They shrugged philosophically, settled into their new home and started raising vegetables in the rich soil. He was unable to obtain steady work in Dawson City because they were not citizens, but she found occasional work on a tour boat.

As with Pete and Mary, the Russos did not appear to be running away. Rather, they were selecting a new way of life with all the care and attention to detail such an ambitious undertaking requires. They were being pragmatic rather than romantic, and unlike so many young people from Outside who want to live in the wilderness, neither couple was a burden on the generosity of other residents. Most important, from old-timers' point of view, they arrived realizing the Yukon is a harsh place for those intent on living off the land and immediately set about finding a way to earn a modest income to offset those things not provided by nature.

Later none of us could remember any features along the last 30 miles to Dawson City because we were so busy watching for the distinctive slide scar on the hill above town. Like the stampeders who frantically paddled and rowed down the river in the early summer of 1898, we had given up on enjoying the scenery and simply wanted to be where we were going. Two weeks in a boat with the same people day and night is a test of patience, and tempers can begin wearing thin, especially during the last two or three days. We learned to appreciate the symptoms of cabin fever that were not present during the gold rush on the passes, but emerged when there was little to do other than steer the boat. Leisure time in boats and cabins breeds discontent, and many of the stampeders stopped speaking to each other before they reached Dawson City and the Klondike goldfields.

So common was the discontent that a sandbar near Fort Selkirk was dubbed "Split-Up Island." Many pairs of stampeders stopped there, unable to bear the thought of four or five more days on the river with their partner, divided their gear and went on alone. These split-ups sometimes were ridiculous in their intensity, with both men refusing to yield. Boats were sawed evenly in two, and sacks of flour and other staples also cut in half.

The men might have had a premonition of what awaited them in the Klondike. Some must have suspected that most, if not all, the good claims would already be staked by early arrivals or, as they were to find, most prospectors who were already in the Yukon drainage flocked in the previous fall and winter to stake them. By no means was the entire stampede stranded on the passes the previous winter. Some of the tougher or the experienced mushed down the river in the dead of winter.

With the possibility of disappointment nagging at them, they became irritable and morose. But in most cases the split-ups were a matter of men living too close too long. The invaluable partner who had saved a man's life or nursed him when he was ill had become a genuine bore—or he showed signs of deep-seated greed or he wiped his nose on his sleeve. Whatever the reason, the stampeders stopped making the laborious diary entries now that they had all the time they needed to make them, and they stopped depending on each other for survival and to reach the Klondike. The common danger was past; they could again be independent and self-sufficient.

After the Klondike gold was discovered, it must have struck some seasoned prospectors as ironic that the most distinctive landmark for a hundred miles in each direction—the slide scar above Dawson City—did not attract them. Like Campbell and the magpie, some must have thought they failed to understand an important omen. It looks like a beacon and cannot be mistaken for any other landmark because there are no other gigantic slide scars along the entire river.

Since 1896 the scar has told river travelers their journey is at an end, and we were no exception as we left that last camp on the last morning and impatiently watched the hills as each river bend opened up the view ahead. We took readings on the fuel and decided we had enough to run full throttle the rest of the way, not regretting the noise because we no longer had anything to say to each other. Conversation could resume after a bath, a trip to a laundromat and a restaurant meal.

Then we saw it, a tan spot that looked like a huge moosehide blanket, much larger than we expected with a wide, curving swath of bare ground where a firebreak had been carved. Barely visible below was the huddle of small buildings that was Dawson City. We were quite pleased with ourselves for covering the entire distance and secretly hoped the first person we met would (1) ask us how far we had come, so that he could (2) be impressed with our saga. Neither of these things happened. We tied up and climbed the bank just as a road grader passed and almost suffocated us with dust.

Far back at the very beginning of our trip we heard a conversation that alerted us to the dangers of trying to impress Yukoners by running the river to Dawson City. A family was taking two boats the entire length of the river, from the headwaters at Lake Bennett to the Bering Sea, and the woman had announced she was writing a book about it and had an assignment with *National Geographic.*

"*National Geographic*, eh?" said a bystander, the "eh" establishing him as Canadian. "They must be planning a hell of an issue on the river. You're the third person I've talked to in the last two days who's 'writing a piece for *National Geo*,' and the second who's writing a book about it."

"Well, I am," she replied defensively and turned her back to him.

Perhaps he had been nursing the grudge for some time, because he bore in on the defeated woman.

"Everybody who comes up here to do the river thinks it's something special. They're all writing books and magazine articles and seem to think they're the first to travel the river— the Magellan Complex. No offense, but we hear the same story every summer—usually from Americans—and we've yet to see a story in *National Geographic* or read a book by someone who traveled the length of the Yukon."

We selected the Downtown Hotel for our quarters because it was nearest the river. We tried to hire a taxi but were told the town's single cab driver was always off somewhere doing something else. We sent an envoy to the Downtown Hotel—who rented our rooms from the bartender in the Sourdough Saloon downstairs—then slung the gear over our shoulders and hiked up and checked in. The hotel occupies the second story, and not one of the rooms has a level floor, all victims of permafrost. Our children soon discovered that not only were the floors slanted, but each room had a different slant. One slanted toward the street, another toward the center of the building and still another away from the others. The children amused themselves by standing coins on edge and watching them roll—and probably lost some money beneath the beds.

There were two bathrooms on the floor, one for each gender, and while our son was taking a bath in an old cast-iron tub an elderly tourist tried to get in. I told him our son was in there and that he could try the rest room downstairs. He interrupted his frantic little dance to glare at me, gave a lunge at the door and ripped off the screw-on hook. With an astonished expression on his face, our son sat stone-still in the soapy water as the old man gained relief.

154

For the tourist (its major source of income now), Dawson City is something of a two-day town. An evening can be spent in the Palace Grand Theater watching English music-hall variety shows and melodramas. The rest of the time can be spent going on the expensive but well-organized guided tours that take most of one day. They run out to Bonanza Creek over a dirt road built atop the dredge tailings and past a few miners still working and reworking claims with a bulldozer, a high-pressure water pump and a big sluice box. They are building their own snakelike tailings as they carve out the gravel hillsides with the hoses, push the gravel into the sluicebox with the dozers and collect the fine flakes of gold.

Some claims have been reworked at least three times—by the original Klondikers, by the Guggenheim interests and again by the present miners. Nobody expects all the gold to ever be taken out of the Bonanza Creek valley or the other nearby streams that have been mined, such as Hunker Creek, Sulphur Creek, Excelsior Creek and the others.

The fabled Mother Lode—from whence came the Klondike gold—has continued to elude prospectors, and most seriously doubt there is such a deposit. Rather, they think the glaciers of the ice ages ground down the rich deposits to the small nuggets and "flour," or very fine gold dust that has always been found there. But the search continues as the hillsides are sluiced out with the hoses until there is virtually no soil left in the valleys—only sand and gravel.

The first miners obviously did not have the sophisticated equipment used today, and their method of sluicing was slower and more miserable. To reach the gold that lay in the ground away from stream beds, they had to dig down as much as thirty feet to bedrock, depending on how far uphill from the stream bed they were. The only way they could get through the permafrost was by building fires in the holes to melt the muck and gravel, then scoop it out to begin all over again. This was usually a wintertime occupation, and they would pile the sand and gravel and mud and gold beside the hole until spring thaw when they could have a "clean-up." Often they would sink the shaft to bedrock, find gold there, then melt the soil off to the side to follow the gold, a process called "drifting." It was a slow, cold and unhealthy occupation, frequently complicated by illnesses ranging from tuberculosis to scurvy. Although Captain James Cook had proved a century earlier that scurvy could be prevented by citrus fruit, and old hands in the north had learned that spruce-needle tea would serve the same function, there were many cases of scurvy before Dawson City was established.

Midnight Dome, a high rounded mountain above the slide scar on the north side of Dawson City, is the nearest thing the Klondike had to a widow's walk. It is here the local people go on June 21, the longest day of the year, to watch the sun not set as it continues its elliptical circuit unfettered by the horizon. It was at the top of Midnight Dome that people once stood to watch for the arrival of the first steamboat, and it is there that people still drive on occasion simply to look at the tiny town below them with the clear water of the Klondike River sweeping out into the muddy Yukon. A trail leads from Dawson City along the edge of the dome and downriver to Moosehide; it is still used occasionally and was once a popular hike for families on a Sunday outing.

Midnight Dome is a strangely moving experience for most who visit it late on a summer night. Like standing beneath the snout of a glacier or watching a storm move across a headwater lake, the ego takes a beating when one is surrounded by the vast wilderness. The town below looks insignificant, almost unnecessary. One knows, while standing on the dome and looking to the north, that there is virtually nothing between there and the Arctic Ocean except more wilderness, that a few miles to the north the tree line ends and the vast tundra begins.

Like the American West, the Canadian government appears intent on bending the Arctic to its will. An example of northward expansion more for the sake of expansion alone than any other reason is a highway being built from near Dawson City to the Arctic Ocean. Called the Dempster Highway, it is being inched northward across the Arctic Circle, across the Richardson Mountains to Fort McPherson on the Peel River in the Northwest Territories. From there it will cross Arctic Red River, then cross the Mackenzie River to Inuvik and continue on north across the absolutely flat tundra and lakes to the

156

Arctic Ocean at a village with the melodious name of Tuk-toyaktuk.

Many Yukoners have second thoughts about the value of the highway now and admit that, while it may help tourism and commerce to some extent (never as much as it is costing to build it), its principal victims are the Eskimos along the Arctic Coast who have been poorly homogenized into the white culture. But the government is committed to the highway; it will be built and lamentations are exercises in futility.

One of the most puzzling paradoxes of the North is the matter of people moving to the wilderness to get away from the trappings of civilization, yet who start importing those same things as soon as they arrive. Like the only child on the block without a ten-speed bike, northerners in the Yukon, as well as over in Alaska, feel they are being deprived if they do not have the amenities found in Vancouver or Toronto or Chicago. The very elements of society which they say drove them to the fringe of civilization are the first things they miss and demand. They cling to the hope that they can import those things that have ruined the wilderness of the more temperate zones, yet control them better.

It is more likely that those attracted to the wilderness are not so enthralled with the wilderness itself as they are with living life on their own terms. Also, many move to the North because they see opportunities to earn large sums of money faster than if they stayed in the provinces. They are the gamblers, the high-risk investors and the merchants who want to get established before the population takes dramatic increases. There are numerous reasons why people move to the Yukon—opportunity, greed, the search for political or social power—but seldom in the interest of preserving the wilderness or establishing an order to the exploitation of mineral resources. With the exception of a few original missionaries and fewer still enlightened bureaucrats, none have expressed concern over the plight of the original inhabitants, the effect the white society is having on them.

Within this context, the Dempster Highway makes perfect sense. Like trips to other planets, construction of the supersonic airplanes and the proliferation of nuclear power plants, these things are possible and for that reason alone should be done. We have not yet learned to admit to ourselves that the technical ability to do something is not enough justification alone for doing it. And, like generations of mankind, one does not necessarily learn from the mistakes of others.

Such musings are not a staple of conversation in the Yukon; to express such opinions there is an invitation to mind one's own bloody business. Conversations in bars are more likely to be on the order of wild experiences, stories of the exploits of local characters, and one's own personal experiences told in something of the "numbskull" tradition of the early Indians. Yukoners, particularly those around Dawson City, tend to be verbal people and good storytellers are highly regarded. With its rich heritage of nonconformists, eccentrics, oddballs and that curious mixture of British formality and frontier vulgarity, the source of rowdy, sometimes bawdy conversation is unlimited.

Tourists riding the boat that runs between Dawson City and Moosehide are given a liberal dose of the storytelling ability, local mythology, and outright tall tales. The boat is owned by one of Dawson City's greatest natural resources, a small, wiry man named Captain Dick Stevenson. He has a hand-rolled cigarette permanently in the corner of his mouth, sometimes lodged in a gap left by a missing tooth. He wears a leather vest with fringing and the words YUKON LOU, the name of his boat and his wife, emblazoned on the back. Few people have ever seen the top of his head because he wears a small, mini-billed motorcycle cap wherever he goes.

Cap'n Dick is not at a loss for great plans. He once wrote out one such plan and mailed it to newspapers on his letterhead, which states the message comes from the River Rat (himself) and at the bottom he added a footnote that says, "It was a beautiful day until some bastard screwed it up."

Cap'n Dick's plan for winter tourism would have delighted Rube Goldberg. He planned to build a wannigan, a house on skids used by logging camps for dining rooms. Then he would pull the wannigan around the wilderness behind a Sno-Cat with a pot-bellied woodstove roaring away to keep the passengers warm and happy while they watched the frozen North glide by the windows. One can easily visualize such a trip as Cap'n Dick pulls the wannigan over rocks and down ravines and hangs it up on stumps amid much colorful cursing in his W. C. Fields, high-pitched, whispery New Brunswickian accent. It would be an adventure only he would enjoy.

His spiel on the riverboat is a delight, too, as he tells why gourds, watermelons and cucumbers do not survive in Dawson City: they grow so fast in the constant sun and rich, black soil that they drag themselves to death. And he says sunflowers will not grow there because they follow the course of the sun and wring their own necks.

He also tells the story, which is true, of two prospectors far out in the wilderness one winter without food. One was certainly dying, and he tried to get his partner to promise he'd eat his body afterward so at least one could live. His partner was horrified and refused. After he died, however, the reluctant partner fed the body to the dog team, then ate the dogs.

Cap'n Dick's finest hour came one summer during the annual Discovery Day celebration, held each August 17 in honor of the date gold was discovered there. It is a rowdy, often mindlessly violent holiday since the highway made access to the town a simple matter of driving three hundred miles. Before that, it was a rather subdued, polite affair with a parade of local families dressed in period costumes and displays of flowers and vegetables. But during the past several years it has become more of a drunken brawl with packs of teenagers, college youths and local Indians drinking in the streets, fighting and savaging the buildings in town. The Mounties dread the celebration almost as much as storekeepers, and the attitude toward police fostered by college students in the United States during the violent 1960s has migrated north with them.

During one Discovery Day celebration, Cap'n Dick had been wading in and around street fights unscathed and with great cheer, and had even thrown a salmon barbecue for a group of friends on an island he owns near Moosehide.

Sometime after the barbecue—he's a little hazy on exact times—he came up with an idea that surpassed any of Robert

Service's practical-joke poems such as the "Ice Worm Cocktail" in which a newcomer (a *cheechako*) was fed noodles in a drink while he thought they were the mythical ice worms.

Cap'n Dick's concoction was called the Sourtoe Cocktail, and he formed the Exalted Order of the Yukon Sourtoe one evening in the Sluicebox bar of the El Dorado Hotel. While it was not a direct insult to the very proper and self-important Yukon Order of Pioneers—Cap'n Dick doesn't have a vicious streak—it is one of those situations that could be so interpreted by those snubbed by the YOP.

When the idea struck, he dashed to his cabin and returned to the Sluicebox with a small black jar and insisted on telling its history before revealing its contents. He said that more than fifty years earlier a local trapper became a rumrunner when Alaska went dry during the Prohibition era. The Yukon remained wet, as usual, so the trapper smuggled liquor across the border by dog team from his cache northwest of Dawson City in the Sixtymile River country. He operated only in the dead of winter when there would be little or no traffic in the wilderness.

During one trip he was caught in a particularly bad storm and froze his feet. He saved everything but one big toe, which he had to amputate himself. Being attached to it emotionally, if no longer physically, he pickled it in a quart of overproof rum and put it on the mantel.

Cap'n Dick said he could understand and appreciate why the trapper had done so: "You've got to understand about winters in the Yukon. When you're all alone in a cabin miles from nowhere for months at a stretch, everything is company, even a big toe in a pickle jar."

It remained in the rum in the jar on the mantel for years. It was still there when Cap'n Dick's prospector wife, Lou, bought the cabin while checking out some mining prospects in the area. The rum had evaporated, but the toe was perfectly preserved.

Now that he had fallen heir to it, he wasn't quite certain what he should do with it. It had a sort of distinction to it, a history, and he was reluctant to haul it out to the cemetery to bury it with the body it came from, and he did not even consider digging an anonymous hole out back somewhere, either. So he kept it until this particular Discovery Day celebration, when the solution came to him "like a bolt of lightning after about ten rounds of beer in the Sluicebox."

He and the bartender, Pete Jenkins, worked out the rules of membership to the EOYS:

Each challenger must give the bartender 12 hours' notice of his intent to order a Sourtoe Cocktail;

No blindfolds allowed, and the drinker must keep his eyes on the toe as it is dropped into a beer glass filled with champagne;

There must be no more than a half inch of champagne left in the glass after the champagne is consumed;

The challenger must stand at the north end of the bar in the light, where everyone can see him or her;

The Sourtoe costs about $10, with contestants having to order a full bottle of champagne for the feat.

The prize? A pat on the back from the bartender, a handshake from the River Rat (Cap'n Dick) and a membership into the Exalted Order of the Yukon Sourtoe.

The "pickled appendage remains behind the bar in a black jar and looks more like a gherkin wearing a hardhat than a petrified toe replete with nail," wrote Dennis Bell in a Canadian Press dispatch on the event. "Stevenson insists the toe is tasteless."

Before he became the first initiate, Stevenson admitted he was a little worried about the monster he was creating. "When I realized I'd have to be the first, my first plan was to get a case of cheap wine, go out into the bush and fortify myself with enough muscatel that anything would taste good after that.

"Instead of that, I just rolled into the bar after work that night, primed myself with three beers and ordered the Sourtoe. Pete performed the rites with his beer glass and silver tongs, and I downed the whole works without thinking twice about it.

"Well," he hedged, "I've got to admit I did feel a little queasy."

If Dawson City had followed the course taken by nearly

every other gold rush town in the North, it would at the most be a roadhouse today, at the least a jumble of rotting boards and broken bottles. But the creeks off the Klondike River still yield enough gold to keep hand miners busy during the summer, and the town has always had a hard core of people who simply would not leave. Many of its residents, some quite elderly, never seriously considered living elsewhere and did not feel compelled to follow the territorial capital south to Whitehorse. Rather than despair and blame the fates or government, they simply stayed and continued business as usual, although there was little remaining to conduct.

It was never quite like any other gold rush town, even though it began its life like one. After George Washington Carmack and his companions in the discovery, Tagish Charley and Skookum Jim, went downriver to Fortymile to register their claims, nearly every creek and settlement between Circle City and Carcross was evacuated before the winter of 1896 set in. It took only a short time for the prospectors and traders to realize that the Klondike River was the bonanza they'd all been looking for over the years. Some miners and traders had been in the middle of the wilderness more than a decade. Trading posts had followed the promising discoveries along the Yukon. Far from any established government, they had lived by rules of their own making, which were sufficient while the population remained small and stable. They lived in tiny, low-ceilinged spruce-log cabins and the saloon–trading posts were their social and legal centers. Their women were Indians, with a few prostitutes who could stand the cold, and a very small number of wives. A steamboat would make perhaps one trip up the river each summer from St. Michaels on the Bering Sea, where provisions from Seattle were dropped off by coastal ships. Often the food was quite rank. Once several dozen seagull eggs collected on the coast were sent upriver in a barrel of seal oil for protection. The porous eggs tasted of the oil, but the men fried them anyway. The traders at Circle City attempted to grow a garden and hitched a team of pet moose to a crude plow. The moose were totally unsatisfactory as draft animals, and the traders had to hire Indians to do the plowing.

Somehow they survived the long wait for the discovery

each man knew was somewhere up the next feeder stream. But when the discovery was made, several of them were already in poor health and few were able to enjoy the end of the search. Joe Ladue, who had a post office trading post and sawmill on Sixtymile Island near Steward Island, is credited with being Dawson City's founder. He packed up all his belongings, drifted down the Klondike River, and set up business again as a real estate salesman, sawmill operator and trader. That first winter of 1896–1897 made him a wealthy man beyond his loneliest winter dream, and he returned to his hometown of Plattsburg, New York, to marry his childhood sweetheart. Only a few months later he heard one of his partners died of tuberculosis enroute Outside. Less than a year after his marriage Ladue, too, was dead of the same disease.

Dawson City's first few years were at once typical of the nineteenth-century gold rush towns, but with its own eccentricities. Unlike the mining towns closer to civilization in Colorado, the Dakotas, Nevada and California, Dawson City had the even and sometimes heavy hand of what was then called the North West Mounted Police. Shysters might cheat each other and a few stampeders be cleaned out in questionable games of chance, but there was virtually no violence and certainly no gunplay. The Mounties were so respected, if not actually feared, that they were simply and completely the law. They administered justice swiftly and humanely. Minor offenders often paid for their transgressions on the post's woodpile by keeping the enormous stack of firewood sufficient to last several winters in advance. One foxy offender, to everyone's delight, carefully cut each stick of firewood a fraction too long to fit into the stove, then left town before he was found out.

The Mounties' control of the rowdy town was an example of a tolerance policy that worked. Gambling was permitted, so were prostitution, B-girls and heavy drinking. But those vices were necessary considering the population and were partaken of in an orderly manner. If that was the way men wanted to spend their fortunes or their low wages, the Mounties believed that was their business. But come Sunday the entire town shut down. There was nothing to do on that day but stroll through town, sleep, write letters, read or even attend church.

The town's isolation was another strong factor in its orderliness; it was a long trip for anyone to make through wilderness to escape. Consequently theft was virtually no problem and there were instances of gold bricks falling off wagons in the middle of town and passersby simply leaving them lay until the mining company came back to get them. In the first place, they were too heavy to pick up and carry off, and even if they were stolen there was no place to convert them into cash.

The town attracted some of the most flamboyant characters in North America in an era that nurtured eccentrics in the English-speaking world. While women in England sometimes wore huge hats filled with tethered, quacking ducks and estates were populated with exotic animals and natives imported as zoo specimens, the Klondike brought out equally unexpected qualities in the men and women there. It was a natural setting for a name-dropping columnist, although apparently none arrived in time to capitalize on it. Had one appeared, the columns would have included such characters as the charming thief and much quoted wit, Wilson Mizner; Swiftwater Bill Gates, a ladies' man extraordinaire and, if not a lucky man in love, certainly one of the luckiest of miners; Diamond Tooth Gertie; Gussie Lamour; Captain Jack Crawford; Jack London; Rex Beech; Joaquin Miller; Arizona Charlie Meadows; and many others.

Dawson City's heyday lasted only about three years, and the Nome gold rush came along conveniently after it was obvious that the best claims were taken around Dawson City. The Nome rush cleared the town of the unemployed and most of the hangers-on who were there to separate the gold from the miners. The population dropped from in excess of 30,000 to around 8,000 in a matter of weeks. One hardy and certainly eccentric stampeder rode a bicycle nearly 2,000 miles over river ice and sandbars from Dawson City to Nome. Nobody thought it particularly odd at the time.

Respectability filled the void left by the evacuation as men with wives and children arrived. It was respectability with a vengeance. Most of the stampeders were Americans, but most of the permanent residents were from Canada, which at that time was more British than North American in attitude. The women brought the strict moral code and the rigid social structure with them. By the time the Guggenheim-backed Yukon Gold Corporation bought all the claims on Bonanza Creek and was dredging it, women were wearing the proper clothing, organizing social clubs and establishing a social structure based, at least in part, on their husbands' position and income.

They had "at-homes," which meant that on specified days the ladies hired a cateress to serve tea, crumpets, muffins and other edibles and other ladies, always wearing white gloves, dropped by for bright chitchat, then went away. It was a social feeling out, a scouting to take inventory of a woman's home and furnishings and her social graces. Should the hostess become indisposed from the vapors or some such ailment, she hung an ornate basket beside the door and didn't answer when the guests knocked. When it was apparent the hostess wasn't going to open up, the guest dropped her calling card in the basket and went away. After the cards were deposited and the coast clear, the indisposed hostess took the calling cards into the house to examine them closely to see how much each lady spent on her cards, and took a census of who came and who did not. It was a mild form of the potlatch—and it let the lady of the house know whom to take seriously in the future. The Canadians explained that this formality, so ridiculed in Noel Coward musicals, was necessary in the wildernesses of the British Empire lest the civilized British subjects "revert."

Despite the influx of respectable ladies and church officials, the prostitutes remained in business over in Klondike City, commonly known as Lousetown, across the Klondike River from Dawson City. They remained there until well beyond the end of the steamboat era, although business by then certainly was not what it once had been. The Mounties and the town's leaders knew the single men needed a sexual outlet and agreed that prostitutes were far superior to having wives and daughters the target or, almost as bad, the Indian women. The respectable women were also saved the discomfort of being continually stared at by the lonely, healthy males. The high, rickety footbridge across the river to Lousetown also provided some of the braver women with amusement: they hid near the bridge in bushes and, tittering, watched to see which men went back and forth across the bridge to consort with the fallen women. Eventually a Dawson City merchant, inspired by a terminal case of do-goodism, caused such a furore in Ottawa over the prostitutes that the Mounties were forced to evacuate them. It was a sad duty and the townspeople helped them move, then so effectively boycotted the merchant that he, too, was forced to leave.

A few hand miners were still at work out on the creeks, but most of the mining after the turn of the century was done by the leviathan dredges, which looked like cranes attached to a warehouse. They were incredibly large—up to four stories tall and more than 100 feet long. They were constructed in stream beds; then the stream was dammed to form a lake on which the dredge floated. They were steam-powered and worked day and night as long as the season permitted, gulping great mouthfuls of gravel laced with gold. After an extraordinary amount of huffing, wheezing, roaring, and rattling, a pitifully small trickle of gold poured through one outlet. From another poured the gravel, which was piled behind in neat mounds of sterile excrement.

One man told of getting a job on a dredge, a machine he had never seen before, and of hearing it long before he saw it. He said it sounded like a carnival with a calliope stranded in the bush with the whistles going, steam spewing out of cylinders, lights going on and off, the crunching and chomping and the men shouting above the din.

When the dredges first began operation the frozen gravel and dirt was thawed with steam points—pipes driven into the permafrost at intervals, then connected to a steam hose that stretched ahead of the dredges from nine different steam plants. The firewood budget for the steam plants was $750,000 for one year alone and cutters had to go farther and farther back into the wilderness for it. Today the spruce are slowly returning to the valleys, but most of the timber is the low-growing, cautious willow bush. After a few years of working with the steam points, a laborious, expensive process, it was discovered that the simpler and faster method of using water from high-pressure hoses did the work better, and whole hillsides were washed down in this manner, sometimes unearthing mastodon bones in the process.

166

For nearly fifty years the dredges slowly ate their way up the streams, until the last of the big deposits were gone. The dredges were left where they were shut down, shipping rates were too high to justify dismantling them for scrap. The nine- or ten-mile tailings wound back and forth behind them as though they were gigantic moles with a sense of neatness burrowing up the valleys, zigzagging back and forth from valley wall to valley wall.

Just after the gold rush, the Yukon Territory was carved off the Northwest Territories with the 60th Parallel as its southern boundary, the 141st Meridian as its western border, and the crest of the Mackenzie Mountains separating it from the Northwest Territories. It was given a small opening onto the Arctic Ocean in the Beaufort Sea. The capital and a number of fine wooden buildings were erected for government offices. A large pseudoplantation-style residence was built for the Commissioner, the federally appointed head of government. This residence was the scene of much pomp and circumstance over the years, and occasional hilarity. Mrs. George Black, a Chilkoot veteran who was married to an early commissioner, wrote of parties in the great ballroom and of guests taking large silver serving platters to the top of the long, open stairway and sliding down the carpeted steps, gay as children on a snowy hill.

Dawson City burned twice during the gold rush era, both times caused by the actions of a prostitute. The first one simply forgot to blow out a candle she left burning in her room; the second threw a lighted lamp at another girl who was becoming too familiar with the prostitute's paramour. Although it put a dent in the businessmen's fortunes, there were still more fortunes to be made then, and it was treated more as a diversion than a catastrophe.

But perhaps the worst blow to befall Dawson City came in the fall of 1918, when many of the Guggenheim employees (called "Guggies") were on their way Outside for visits after dredging operations were shut down. They went by the last steamboat of the season to Whitehorse, then by train to Skagway, and boarded the elegant Canadian Pacific steamer *Sophia*. When she left the Skagway pier, 343 were aboard including the crew, and the first evening out she ran aground on a reef between Skagway and Juneau. The captain was not worried and told the captain of another ship who came to offer assistance that she was in no danger and that she would float free when the next tide came in. The *Sophia* stayed on the reef all night, and the next morning a storm blew her off the reef, tearing a hole in her bottom. She quickly sank, and everyone aboard died.

Most of the passengers were from Dawson City—with the exception of the owner of the Carcross parrot—and the tragedy reduced the town's population by nearly a third. Its survivors say the town never really recovered. The dredges kept working, but in the winter the town was virtually dead. In 1951 the population was down to 783, while Whitehorse had grown, courtesy of the Alaska Highway, to 9,096. It was obvious to everyone that the capital would soon be moved to the south and that the steamboats were also on the endangered list. The last session of the territorial council was held in Dawson City the next year.

The town's only links with Outside were the telegraph lines that followed the river to Whitehorse, then down through the interior of British Columbia, and the old winter road. The winter road was a rough right-of-way slashed and scooped out of the timber along the edges of mountains over which open sleds and wagons were pulled by horses from freezeup to breakup. Sleds were used when the snow was deep; wagons during the first and last part of each winter.

The stages operated until the temperature fell to minus 40 degrees, where it was unsafe for horses to work without freezing their lungs. Passengers were provided charcoal foot warmers and great buffalo robes. Regular travelers had coonskin caps they used especially for the stage trips and left them on pegs in the Whitehorse office when not in use. Some women passengers complained about men whose hands wandered about beneath the robes as though they had minds of their own while the owner's face bore no suggestion of the activities beneath the robes. Should a woman complain, the owner of the offending hand, being a British subject, would usually reply with great and injured dignity that the lady must be mistaken.

The sled stages were large enough for fourteen people,

including the driver, and teams of four to six horses were used to pull them. They could travel 60 miles on a good day, changing horses at every roadhouse, and the 300-mile trip took from five to seven days. The sleds also had small stoves that burned constantly so that perishable freight would not freeze and menu items in Dawson City often were listed as "Over the Ice," meaning they had arrived by stage with the heaters keeping them edible.

Toward the end of the roadless era the horses were replaced by Caterpillar tractors and Dawson City was served by the "Cat trains." During all this time the confirmed Yukoners clung to Dawson City, sometimes with desperation, rather than moving to the uninteresting and upstart town of Whitehorse. Most believed Whitehorse should have remained a steamboat dock and railroad station and would have done so had it not been for the nonsense of World War II and the bloody highway project.

Even a few of the madams remained loyal to Dawson City men in their fashion. Two or three madams were permitted to operate on a very small scale—modest rooming houses and a private home. Those who stayed were still called girls although they had the disquieting habit of dying off one by one of old age. They were as much a part of the Dawson City scenery as the slide scar above town and the baseball games that start promptly at midnight on June 21 each year. Residents still speak of them with warmth and humor, although any attempt by a woman to go into that business now is quickly and politely rebuffed by the Mounties. One of the former madams, who would have been ancient by most people's standards, was still quite capable of entertaining an occasional old customer in her parlor. A respectable woman called on her one afternoon about a community matter and received no answer when she knocked on the door. She heard someone shouting inside the house and thought perhaps the old whore had fallen and hurt herself. She opened the door and entered and heard more shouts coming from upstairs. The visitor followed the sounds and peeked in the bedroom door. There on the bed lay the old madam in all her faded glory, nude and spread-eagled. In a bathtub near the bed sat an elderly man, also nude and obviously very drunk, pretending he was rowing the bathtub on a sylvan lake with the madam shouting: "Row, you son of a bitch! Row that boat!" The visitor left quickly and quietly.

The same madam once bought a dress on the installment plan at a local dry-goods store, paying a small amount—perhaps $5 a week—over a period of months. When she came into the store one frigid day with the last payment, the storekeeper told her he would wrap it for her.

"I'll wear it," she said, and took off her long fur coat. She was stark naked. She slipped the dress over her head, reached back to zip it, put on her fur coat and went home.

Building on permafrost requires techniques none of the Dawson City architects knew, and the town was put up as though it were in Nevada. The foundations lay on top of the ground, sometimes on stone but usually on blocks of wood that last almost indefinitely in the dry climate. But the trouble comes in the summer when the ground thaws down about a foot, then freezes up again in the fall. This alternating freeze and thaw shifts the foundations and gives the houses decided lists. After one brick building split neatly in half this construction material was abandoned.

While houses were occupied the owners made corrections to keep them on an even keel. But after Dawson City was almost abandoned the houses were permitted to bulge and tilt at will. They lean tiredly against each other or sag in the middle until no windows or doors are on the same level.

The first task of the historic preservation crews is to correct the leans and lists with hefty screw-jacks and sturdy wooden foundations. When work began on the old post office building, more than eighty jacks were placed beneath it. New buildings are placed either on a 2- or 3-foot gravel pad to permit water runoff and air circulation, or steel piling is driven deep into the ground to let the permafrost hold them firmly in place.

The permafrost creates other problems as well, one of which plagued the town's undertaker years ago. In order to dig graves in a sensible manner, he had to hire them dug during the summer months, and even then it was no easy task. Like the miners out on the creeks, the thawed topsoil could be scraped off easily enough, but the frozen ground beneath had to be thawed by building a fire, scooping out the thawed muck, and building more fires until bedrock was reached in the miners' case—or 6 feet for the undertaker.

The undertaker had to have a sharp eye and a gambler's instinct when digging them because his clients were still alive. Each summer he took a general reading of the old-timers and guessed how many would die before the following summer and hired diggers accordingly.

One autumn an old-timer was seen trudging down the street to catch the last steamboat out to Whitehorse. Ahead of the old gentleman was the town's handyman, hauling the baggage in a wheelbarrow. The undertaker saw him and was deeply distressed. He ran after him, pleading that the old man stay. He had dug a grave for him the previous summer and now, to his horror, the potential occupant was leaving.

The undertaker tried to convince the old man that he should stay in Dawson City; all his friends were there, his belongings were there and he might go Outside and die among strangers. The old man kept walking steadily toward the dock behind the handyman, and just as steadily the undertaker followed and begged and pleaded. The steamboat skipper saw them coming and was irritated by the undertaker's gall. He picked up the bullhorn and climbed to the top deck.

"Leave him alone, you son of a bitch! If he wants to leave the country, that's his business," he shouted loud enough for most of the town to hear.

The undertaker faltered, then stopped and sadly watched his client-to-be slowly, carefully walk up the ramp aboard the steamboat. His assessment was accurate: the old man died that winter, Outside.

Most of the elderly men chose to stay in Dawson City and die there, though. The Sisters of St. Ann, who were sent to Dawson City during the gold rush to care for the sick and to raise crops of vegetables on islands in the river, operated a hospital and nursing home for a number of years in Dawson

City. They were noted for their respect for the old men and tried to operate the nursing home for the benefit of those living there.

Perhaps the saddest event of each year was the departure each October of the last steamboat before freeze-up. More than the short days and the plummeting thermometer, this meant the winter isolation was beginning. Usually it was a pseudo-festive occasion with parties lasting all the previous night and passengers and crew alike staggering aboard the boat for the three-day, sometimes dangerous trip back to Whitehorse on the shallow river. Often the paddlewheelers traveled in pairs to assist each other when one went aground, and to race whenever possible on the broader, deeper stretches of river and across Lake Laberge. But for Dawson City it was a time of sadness, even though many preferred the almost hibernation pace of the winter months. Most of the town would stand on the river bank watching as the steamboats moved slowly away from the dock with friends waving handkerchiefs, then cut across the eddy created by the Klondike River into the swift water of the river and finally around the bend and out of sight until the following June. The winter stages would begin running before long but they were poor substitutes for the steamboats.

Winter often brought short tempers and controversies bred of confinement. It is a joke among the more stable Yukoners to wonder what the arguing will be about the coming winter, and when a local controversy erupts during the summer, it usually takes them by surprise. A few years ago when almost the entire city council of Whitehorse resigned in protest over federal intervention in city affairs, one member wondered aloud why they hadn't waited until winter for the political brawl.

Dawson City has had its share of manufactured controversies, some of which take unexpected turns toward resolution. One winter the problem was the city water supply. Since it is expensive to have running water because of freezing pipes that ran from the Klondike River to town, nearly everyone depended on a water wagon for delivery and paid $12 a month for the service. A quarrel started over the price, and a town meeting was held to discuss this outrageous charge. During the protest meeting one citizen stood and calmly told them that he didn't think that was such a terrible price to pay someone else to go out and get cold while chopping a hole in the river and pumping water. He said he would gladly pay $25 a month for the service. The meeting became absolutely silent after his presentation, then a buzz went through the audience and in a matter of minutes they voted unanimously to increase the price to $25.

It was Canada's growing sense of nationalism and a pride in its heritage that saved much of Dawson City from gracelessly falling in on itself. This pride combined with the growing tourist industry led to the current restoration program that first saved the old Palace Grand Theater. It dated back to 1899 when Arizona Charlie Meadows built it to be the most ornate and elegant theater north of Vancouver, B.C. It was almost gone, a victim of time and neglect, before the Dawson City businessmen formed the Klondike Visitors Association, somehow raised $750,000 in private capital to match a $650,000 grant from the federal government to restore the building. Part of the program also involved bringing the steamboat *Keno* down from Whitehorse to be beached and turned into a museum.

With all the restoration work completed, the new Palace Grand was opened with the premier of the Way-Off-Broadway production of *Foxy*, starring Bert Lahr. The festival built around Lahr's presence brought 18,000 people into town, the most since June 1899, when most of the out-of-work-and-luck miners left for Nome or the Spanish-American War.

The restoration is still in progress with some two dozen of the old, false-front buildings selected as part of the Klondike Gold Rush International Historical Park.

The Canadian government isn't being puritanical about the restoration. One of the former bawdy houses has been selected and now stands chastely on a wooden platform waiting for a permanent foundation. It is a small, two-story building with bulging bay windows and was last called Ruby's Place. Ruby called it a rooming house and told people all those young ladies who moved in and out over the years were her relatives, nieces and cousins, who came to visit for varying lengths of time.

The Klondike Highway that runs north from Whitehorse continues across the Yukon River by ferry and swings west to follow the crests of low, rounded mountains to Fairbanks, Alaska. Except for the brief tourist season most of the highway traffic is the large diesel trucks that haul asbestos ore from the Clinton Creek Mine near Fortymile to the railroad at Whitehorse.

The toll-free ferry runs back and forth almost around the clock between breakup and freeze-up. The mine operates the year around and tall steel towers on either side of the river with heavy cable slung between them haul the trucks back and forth like gondola cars during periods of unstable ice. After the river freezes, water is pumped onto the ice to increase its normal thickness to 10 or 12 feet so it will support the heavy trucks.

Dawson City becomes very lonely during the winter, and as with most towns in the north with a tourist industry, many of the businessmen migrate south, taking the money earned there elsewhere to be spent. The streets become virtually deserted and an ice fog often hangs over town, blotting out the sun during its short appearance. Temperatures of minus 50 degrees and lower are common and expected.

When people must take an automobile out in that weather, they either keep the engine running constantly or make frequent trips out to start the engine, let it warm up, then turn it off again and go back inside. During parties guests sometimes set an alarm clock to remind themselves to start the car, put on their parkas and mittens and go out to sit in the car until it is warm again, then return to the party. Every car is equipped with an engine-block heater that is plugged into electrical outlets, and they can only hope the uncertain power system doesn't go out during the night. Some cars are kept running for days, weeks even, and all over the towns of the North they are left idling while people shop.

While newer homes, particularly those built by the federal government for the growing Indian population of Dawson City, have modern insulation and central heating, most of the Dawson City homes are quite elderly and of frame construction. They are not well insulated, and stoves are kept burning con-

174

stantly with thick drapes over the windows, quilts and blankets over doors and thick rugs on the floor. Some families close off rooms and let them turn into refrigerators during the winter. In spite of wood or oil stoves burning all night, bedrooms turn viciously cold and people sometimes wake with frost on their face or with their hair painfully frozen to the headboard.

Yet the people, some of whom could well afford to migrate like waterfowl, stay. Some couples move away from the Yukon to retire, but those who do usually keep in close touch with other Yukoners, like World War II bomber crews or survivors of disasters at sea. After living in the Yukon a few years, those who leave can never treat it as casually as though they had lived in Manitoba or Alberta. They have survived the summer thunderstorms and the big dark of the winters. They do not necessarily believe they themselves are special—but they are certain they have experienced something special.

Yet they do not care to be called heroic. One couple retired from Dawson City to Idaho, but soon were back in Dawson City because they resented being treated like exotics and being invited to parties so people could meet "that interesting couple who lived in the North." It was the experiences they survived that were interesting, they thought, certainly not themselves.

A first-time visitor in Dawson City who had met several of the longtime residents and was sitting in the Sluicebox talking with Cap'n Dick Stevenson about that serenity so common among them commented that there seemed to be no way to really impress the old-timers, other than with the old-fashioned virtues of truth and honor and fair play.

"That's right," said Stevenson, "not unless you learn to walk on water."

So the people stay in Dawson City, not to get rich or escape the realities of Outside or because they like the risk of freezing a nose or finger or toe every winter. They stay for the same reasons people live in humid, uncomfortable cities with dangerous streets, and the same reasons people live on farmland so poor it will hardly grow weeds. The Yukoners stay because it is what they know, what they are accustomed to and, in the case of Dawson City, what they have grown to love more than any other place they know.

Epilogue

The river is redundant beyond Dawson City. It continues its silent, northward rush but soon becomes an Alaskan river in the flat, repetitive, mosquito-infested Yukon Flats up where the tree line and tundra merge in the maze of slack water and dead-end sloughs. But for me the Yukon ends at Dawson City: beyond, it becomes a statistical appendix.

It appears inevitable that more dams will be built on the river just as more of the landscape will be pock-marked with mines as man, for his own reasons, emulates the beaver and the bear. The lightning fires that sweep the stunted spruce forests each summer like plagues will continue burning more wood than the steamboats ever did. Human nature, one of the constants of the universe, will not permit the vast wilderness to remain unchanged, and our graffiti will multiply until the next Ice Age flattens and smoothes and rearranges the land again. Then, when the ice retreats back to the Beaufort Sea and mountaintops, and leaves new valleys and river courses, the cycle will begin again.